Critical Questions, Critical Perspectives: Language and the Second Language Educator

a volume in
Contemporary Language Studies in Education

Series Editor: Terry A. Osborn

Contemporary Language Studies in Education

Terry A. Osborn, Series Editor

Teaching Language and Content to Linguistically and Culturally Diverse Students: Principles, Ideas, and Materials (2004)
by Yu Ren Dong

Early Language Learning: A Model for Success (2004)
by Carol M. Saunders Semonsky & Marcia A. Spielberger

Critical Questions, Critical Perspectives: Language and the Second Language Educator

by

Timothy Reagan

Roger Williams University

INFORMATION AGE PUBLISHING

Greenwich, Connecticut • www.infoagepub.com

Library of Congress Cataloging-in-Publication Data

Reagan, Timothy G.
Critical questions, critical perspectives : language and the second language educator / by Timothy Reagan.
p. cm. -- (Language studies in education)
Includes bibliographical references.
ISBN 1-59311-334-X (pbk.) -- ISBN 1-59311-335-8 (hardcover)
1. Language and languages--Study and teaching. 2. Second language acquisition. 3. Linguistic minorities. 4. Education, Bilingual. 5. Multicultural education. I. Title. II. Series.
P53.R4 2005
418'.0071--dc22

2005004482

Printed in the United States of America

This one is for Jo Ann

CONTENTS

PREFACE

Critical Questions, Critical Perspectives: Language and the Second Language Educator is intended primarily for language educators, broadly conceived, and thus is appropriate for not only foreign language teachers, but also individuals teaching English to speakers of other languages in both Anglophone and non-Anglophone settings, teachers in bilingual education programs, heritage language teachers in both formal and informal settings, and others whose work involves language teaching and learning. It is also intended for teachers of all age groups and levels, since the issues that it raises are neither age nor level specific. This is not a book about teaching methodology, nor is it the sort of work that will provide the teacher with practical activities for use in the classroom. There are many other books that are of these types, and they are valuable and worthwhile for what they are intended to do (see, for example, J. Davis & Osborn, 2003; Hall, 2001; Omaggio Hadley, 2001; Osborn, in press; Richard-Amato, 1996; Shrum & Glisan, 1994; Ur, 1996).

This book is deliberately different. It is not concerned with issues of teaching, methods, assessment, management, and so on, in classroom contexts. Rather, it asks the language educator to step back from his or her daily challenges and concerns and consider some of the many important theoretical issues that underlie and inform our pedagogy and profession. Specifically, *Critical Questions, Critical Perspectives: Language and the Second Language Educator*, as its title suggests, takes a critical perspective on many of the common practices and assumptions of our profession. It challenges us to reflect on our practice, and it asks us to explore a number of important questions about language teaching and learning more broadly and fully than we have perhaps done in the past: questions like what we mean by *language*, how one *learns* language, why students ought to study a second language, and so on. It also seeks to put the teaching and learning of languages in a social, political, and ideological context, and tries to demonstrate the role played in language education by these various extralinguistic factors.

Critical Questions, Critical Perspectives: Language and the Second Language Educator consists of seven chapters. The title of each of the seven chapters begins with a question, around which the chapter is organized and to which it seeks to provide, not so much an answer, as guidance for how an answer might be conceptualized. Thus, the seven questions around which the book has been written include:

- Does language really exist?
- What does it mean to know a language?
- Why study a second/foreign language?
- Who decides which language?
- Why can't I take Russian at school?
- Language learning and feelings of disgust?
- Where have all the languages gone?

Some of these questions are quite clear, while others may need a bit of an explanation. In fact, taken together they seek to raise questions about a wide range of issues related to language education and the relationship between language education and social justice—questions with which, I believe, every language educator needs to grapple (see also Hafernik, Messerschmitt, & Vandrick, 2002).

Several of the chapters included in this book have appeared in earlier forms elsewhere, and I am grateful for the permission to update and expand them. I have also been blessed with a number of incredibly bright, talented and insightful colleagues, with whom I have had the opportunity to discuss many of the ideas found in this book is great detail. In particular, I want to thank Christine Brown, Barbara Lindsey, Frank Nuessel, Terry A. Osborn, Linda Pelletier, Claire Penn, Sharon Rallis, Xaé Reyes, Eliana Rojas, Sandra Schreffler, and Humphrey Tonkin for their help and support. And, as always, special thanks for everything to Jo Ann, Joshua, Bryan, and Kimberly.

CHAPTER 1

DOES LANGUAGE REALLY EXIST?

An Introduction to Critical Language Study

An attempt to define any language (such as English, Swahili, Tagalog) or variety of language (such as Cockney, Brooklynese, Hawai'ian Creole) will always be confounded by political and cultural complications.

— *Rosina Lippi-Green* (2000, p. 232)

Language matters. This is hardly a radical claim for a second/foreign language educator to make, of course, and yet, in this chapter I want to suggest that while language *does* matter, it is also the case that what this phrase actually means is incredibly complex and problematic. The term *language* is one which we use all of the time, but its semantic content is quite often neither clear nor particularly useful. Indeed, I want to suggest here that the term language is often used in a nonreflective manner that actually leads to misunderstandings and misrepresentations both of the nature of human language in general and of second/foreign language teaching and learning in particular. As Terry A. Osborn has compellingly argued, contemporary language teacher education is based, in large part, on four fundamental assumptions: that language can be presented as an *objective* reality, that the language user can meaningfully be separated from the language, that generalizations and observations regarding language teaching can be presented free from situational and temporal con-

Critical Questions, Critical Perspectives:
Language and the Second Language Educator, 1–16

straints, and finally, that learning to teach a language is a value-free (technicist) process (2004, pp. 274-275). These assumptions are all grounded in generally unarticulated epistemological assumptions that are themselves questionable, and alternative epistemologies are available to us which are arguably far better suited to the realities of understanding second/foreign language teaching and learning.

THE LEGACY OF LOGICAL POSITIVISM

Among the more interesting intellectual debates of the twentieth century was that which took place among philosophers of science and others interested in understanding both the nature and limits of human knowledge. These efforts reached a peak in the 1920s with the work of a group of philosophers known as the Vienna Circle (*Wienerkreis*), and building on the philosophical foundation provided by Descartes, Leibniz, and others, logical positivism provided a framework for the development of an approach to epistemology that dominated philosophical discourse, at least in the Anglophone world, well into the 1960s (see Audi, 1998), and continues to exert considerable influence in many disciplinary fields. Positivism, in its simplest form, basically presupposes the existence of an external reality that we can seek to recognize and understand. Reality is thus singular, divisible, and, to some extent, knowable. It is knowable through the use of common methods of observation and public confirmation. Science, and by extension all intellectual activity, therefore has as its goal the articulation and, ultimately, the control (albeit in necessarily limited ways) of this singular reality.

Linguists and language specialists, as well as the general public, have tended to view language from a perspective that is, at its heart, fundamentally positivist in orientation. We have tended to assume that language as an abstract entity, in a Chomskian sense,[1] exists as just such a knowable entity. As Neil Smith has noted,

> There is an intuitive appeal to the notion that there is an external language that different people speak. Indeed, it is so self-evidently true that it would be pointless to deny it. However, when taken to its logical conclusion, the idea turns out to be problematic, as the notion of "language" involved is different from the notion that linguists theorize about. (2002, p. 103)

Even more problematically, we have assumed that not only does language exist, but further, that *particular* languages also exist as knowable entities which can be described and analyzed. Such assumptions and presuppositions are embedded in our discourse, and in turn have important implications for applied language studies. We commonly make claims about English, French, Spanish, German, Russian, Arabic, Japanese, Xhosa, and so on, just as we make claims about the nature of human language in more general terms. Indeed, when we engage in the teaching of second/foreign languages, our goal is to move the student's linguistic behavior in the second language closer to the preconceived norms of the singular reality of that target language. What we do, in short, is (1) to engage in the objectification of the construct of language, which in turn (2) leads us to misunderstand the nature of language and (3) to accept technicist views of the teaching and learning of languages. Underlying all of this is, ultimately, the effort to make language and language use controllable—whether for the native or second/foreign language learner.

The deeper one pursues the everyday conception of language, the fuzzier and more problematic the concept seems to become. As Ronald Wardhaugh has commented,

> Language plays an important role in the lives of all of us and is our most distinctive human possession. We might expect, therefore, to be well-informed about it. The truth is we are not. Many statements we believe to be true about language are likely as not false. Many of the questions we concern ourselves with are either unanswerable and therefore not really worth asking or betray a serious misunderstanding of the nature of language. Most of us have learned many things about language from others, but generally the wrong things. (1999, p. viii)

In its most commonplace and everyday uses, however, the conception of language is both ahistorical and atheoretical. It is ahistorical in that it presupposes that language is in some sense (especially in educational contexts) fixed and static; that is, that it is a singular reality, in positivistic terms. Consider the case of English. The speech community of English has evolved over the past thousand years in a variety of ways. From a relatively small and insignificant linguistic community on the fringe of Europe, English speakers have become the single most powerful linguistic community in the world, albeit a highly diverse and to some extent factionalized linguistic community (see Brutt-Griffler, 2002; Crystal, 2003; Durand, 2001; McArthur, 1998). The domination and near-hegemony of English in international communication is unmatched in the history of our species, and presents serious threats to both cultural and linguistic diversity (see Brutt-Griffler, 2002; Crystal, 2003; Holborow, 1999; Phillipson, 2003; Sonntag, 2003; Tonkin & Reagan, 2003). Not only has English spread, though, but it has also evolved and changed in dramatic ways. In fact, we normally distinguish among Old English, Middle English, and Modern English, and consider each of these a distinctive language in its own right (see Barber, 1993; Burrow & Turville-Petre, 1996; Leith, 1997; Mitchell & Robinson, 1992; J. Smith, 1999). The very fact of such linguistic evolution, incidentally, provides compelling evidence about the dangers and risks of seeing language as static and fixed. Certainly a speaker of Modern English finds Old English unintelligible, regardless of the historical connections between the two. And yet, the demarcation of each of these separate languages is in fact arbitrary—there is no point at which speakers of Old English suddenly began speaking Middle English. There was a continuity in the English speaking linguistic community throughout the past thousand years, and at no point were native speakers of one generation unable to understand native speakers of the next generation. The same, of course, is true of the evolution of the Romance languages from Latin, and would be true of any case of linguistic evolution. From a strictly historical perspective, *any* language is thus something of a moving target. Codification, of course, can and does slow this process down, but it does not prevent it. Language—*any* language—is constantly changing and in flux, and thus any effort to demarcate the boundaries of a particular language are inevitably at best able to provide a snapshot of the language at a particular time and place. A fairly good analogy is provided by the coastline of Britain; we all know that there *is* such a thing, and can talk about it and even show pictures of it—and yet, it really does not exist except as an abstraction. The waves at the edge of the coast, and the coastline itself, are constantly in a state of flux. In a sense, it is simply not possible to measure the coastline since it is always changing. The same is true of the concept language. At the same time, of course, we can and do create rough approximations of the coastline of Britain, just as we can and do create rough approximations of particular languages.

Conceptions of language are not only ahistorical, though, they are also atheoretical in nature. Language varies, as we all know, not only over time, but also from place to place, social class to social class, and individual to individual. Ekkehard Wolff, in a discussion of the relationship of language and society in the African context, has noted that, "no two speakers of the same language speak alike, nor does the same speaker use his/her language the same way all the time: variation is part of language and language behaviour" (2000, p. 299). As Rebecca Posner has noted in her response to the question, "How many Romance languages are there?":

> An answer to this question that has been slightingly labeled *santa simplicitas* is that there is only one: the languages are all alike enough to be deemed dialects of the same language. Another equally disingenuous answer might be "thousands"—of distinctive varieties—or "millions"—of individual idiolects. The usual textbook answer is "ten, or possibly eleven", according priority to putative chronologically early differentiation from the common stock, allegedly linked to ethnic differences among the speakers. (1996, p. 189)

Posner's point is well taken: even in a case as well documented as that of the Romance languages, the specific demarcation of distinct languages is fundamentally an arbitrary one. We see this same problem in delimiting languages in settings around the world. Although the criterion of mutual intelligibility is useful in some instances, it is far from adequate in many others. Norwegian, Swedish, and Danish have a very high degree of mutual intelligibility, and yet are recognized, both by their speakers and by others, as different languages. In distinguishing between *languages* and *dialects*, we are ultimately left with the distinction attributed to Max Weinreich: "The difference between a language and a dialect is who's got the army and navy."

This is not at all a small matter, though it is not the whole story. Language boundaries are determined not so much by linguistic criteria, but rather by extralinguistic criteria, as was suggested by Weinreich. Furthermore, since no two speakers of a language possess and use the language in identical ways—indeed, since no *single* speaker does so—we are left with the reality of language as existing only in the plural. A language, in short, is ultimately a collection of idiolects which have been determined to belong together for what are ultimately non- and extralinguistic reasons. The writers who have suggested that we need to speak of English*es,* rather than of English, are correct as far as they go (see, for example, Bamgbose, Banjo, & Thomas, 1997; Kachru, 1982; McArthur, 1998)—but they do not go quite far enough. Not only are there multiple English*es*, but there are quite literally millions of different Englishes, both in a global context and in our own national context. Nor does this observation apply solely to English; it is true of each and every language. There are French*es*, Russian*s*, and Navajo*s*, but no English, French, Russian or Navajo.

IMPLICATIONS FOR SECOND/FOREIGN LANGUAGE EDUCATION

The ahistorical and atheoretical conceptualization of language has important implications for the teaching and learning of languages. By objectifying the construct of language as a single entity, we inevitably oversimplify and reify not only language itself, but also the components of language and the related skills and concepts related to language teaching and learning. The grammar of a language becomes what is contained in a textbook or reference grammar; the lexicon becomes synonymous (more or less) with what is in the dictionary. Of course, taken to its extreme, this argument becomes unworkable—in precisely the same way that it is difficult to set specific or exact parameters on *day* and *night,* while yet granting that both concepts are meaningful, so too does language exist in concept if not in detail. This is nonetheless important, though, since in the classroom context, the second/foreign teacher often becomes the final, ultimate language authority and model for his or her students. As Barbara Craig has commented,

> Traditionally, the [second/foreign language] teacher's role has been seen as that of an authoritative expert. This view is based on the conception of knowledge as a quantifiable intellectual commodity. The teacher, as an expert in a field of inquiry or as an expert speaker of a language, has more of this knowledge than his or her students have. Because this knowledge has a separate existence outside of its knowers, it can be given, or taught, to the learners by the teacher-expert. (1995, p. 41)

Indeed, the second/foreign language educator becomes the ultimate authority on the language being taught not only for his or her students, but also often for colleagues and superiors who do not speak the target language. Although it is obviously absurd, it is far from uncommon in the U.S. context to find the performance of second/foreign language educators being evaluated by individuals who do not themselves speak the target language being taught.

The objectification of language is, then, ultimately about power (see Fairclough, 1989; Reagan, 2001a, 2002b; Tollefson, 1995). It is about who has the power to determine standards of correctness, and about who is entitled to *ownership* of the language. The selection of a particular variety of the target language as the norm in the second/foreign language classroom is a manifestation of the ideology of linguistic legitimacy. In a nutshell, the ideology of linguistic legitimacy presupposes that some language varieties are more legitimate than others, and that some languages are more *real* than others (see Reagan, 1997b). This is perhaps nowhere clearer than in the case of heritage and native language speakers in the second/foreign language classroom. As Valdés has noted,

> it is a fact that a surprising number of Spanish-speaking students … are still being placed in beginning Spanish classes for non-speakers to help them "unlearn" their "bad" habits and begin anew as foreign speakers. It matters not that the student is fluent and has internalized every single grammar rule that the teacher may hope to present. If he says *traiba* for *traía*, many schools will make him "begin from the beginning" … every day teachers of Spanish casually enroll native Spanish-speaking students in beginning Spanish classes for non-speakers, in which the materials used have been designed exclusively for teaching English-speaking students. The students are expected, in the process, to acquire the standard Spanish dialect as opposed to that normally used in their own speech communities. (1981, p. 7)

Power relations with respect to language variation are not, though, limited only to the second/foreign language classroom. The not uncommon tension between bilingual education teachers and foreign language teachers is often a reflection of different linguistic norms and the status differentials between the standard and the nonstandard varieties of the language. There is also at issue here the difference between perceptions of second/foreign language education as an enrichment educational activity for native speakers of the socially dominant language (English) and perceptions of bilingual education for speakers of other languages as remedial. The difference between a speaker of Spanish who uses *troca* and one who uses *camión* for truck is, in short, not simply one of lexical choice; it is, rather, one of class, status, power, and context.

The objectification of language is reflected in the objectification of a number of other related constructs as well: not only grammar and vocabulary, but also that of the native speaker, culture, communication, performance, production, literacy, and so on. Consider, for instance, the concept bilingual. Although we would all recognize that this term actually refers to a very diverse continuum of different levels and types of language skills in two or more languages, efforts to provide a single, clear definition for bilingual are bound to fail (see Wei, 2000). In fact, definitions of bilingualism range from very strong versions to remarkably weak ones. The following definitions, all taken from the relevant research literature and all reflected in our everyday discourse, make clear just how broad the determination of what constitutes bilingualism can be:

- The individual has nativelike proficiency in two languages.
- The individual can use two languages alternately.
- The individual can produce meaningful sentences in the second language.
- The individual can engage in communication in more than one language.
- The individual possesses at least one language skill (listening, speaking, reading, or writing) in a second language to a minimal degree.
- The individual can use a passive knowledge of a second language and a little lexical competence to transact business in the second language. (Ovando, Collier, & Combs, 2003, p. 165).

To be sure, some of these definitions are so broad as to make the concept of bilingualism virtually meaningless, while others would result in the exclusion of the vast majority of individual speakers who consider themselves, and are considered by others, to be bilingual. The point here is that there is no single, agreed-upon conception of what, precisely, is meant by bilingual. Indeed, if one examines the actual use of this term in the public school context in the United States, one is left with the paradoxical discovery that the children who are bilingual (and who are therefore in bilingual education programs of various sorts) are those who do not yet speak English proficiently; once they are able to function in English, by some mysterious alchemy they are no longer labeled bilingual in the public school context. To be sure, this is an especially odd use of the term, but it is nevertheless a common one, and again, it reflects not issues of language and linguistics, but rather issues of power, domination, and hegemony.

LANGUAGE, POWER AND IDEOLOGY

The objectification of language leads to technicist approaches to teaching language, in which assumptions are made about the correctness of particular language varieties and linguistic forms, as well as about the relationship between the hypothetical native speaker, the people who actually speak the target language, and the second language user. Technicism, in essence, is the tendency to address complex social, political, economic, ideological, and educational issues as merely technical problems requiring technical solutions. It is ultimately concerned with matters of control. As Lourdes Ortega has recently commented, the teaching of second/foreign languages in the United States has failed "to recognize the fact that both societal attitudes towards languages and power struggles resulting from ownership of a language and culture by particular groups are inextricably embedded in the definition of goals for language education" (1999, p. 243). Not only does technicism result in poor language teaching, but even more significantly, it serves to disguise the very real political and ideological contexts in which language learning occurs. A number of scholars in recent years have critically assessed this tendency in the international teaching of English (see Hall & Eggington, 2000; Holborow, 1999; Pennycook, 1994, 1998). Robert Phillipson, for instance, has argued that the belief that English language teaching is somehow a nonpolitical or nonideological activity:

> serves to *disconnect culture from structure.* It assumes that educational concerns can be divorced from social, political, and economic realities. It exonerates the experts who hold the belief from concerning themselves with these dimensions. It encourages a technical approach to [English language teaching], divorced even from wider educational issues. It permits the English language to be exported as a standard product without the requirements of

> the local market being considered except in a superficial way. (1992, p. 67, emphasis in original)

In fact, the role of English in the international community is far from neutral or nonideological; as Chris Searle has argued,

> Let us be clear that the English language has been a monumental force and institution of oppression and rabid exploitation throughout 400 years of imperialist history. It attacked the black person with its racist images and imperialist message, it battered the worker who toiled as its words expressed the parameters of his misery and the subjugation of entire peoples in all the continents of the world. It was made to scorn the languages it sought to replace, and told the colonised peoples that mimicry of its primacy among languages was a necessary badge of their social mobility as well as their continued humiliation and subjugation. Thus, when we talk of "mastery" of the Standard language, we must be conscious of the terrible irony of the word, that the English language itself was the language of the master, the carrier of his arrogance and brutality. (1983, p. 68)

What is especially intriguing in this admittedly polemical passage is that even as he is attacking the technicist view of language, Searle inadvertently falls into the trap of objectifying English—indicating that the problem is in fact frighteningly contagious. It is not, after all, *English* that did anything—speakers of English, and political institutions representing the power and self-interest of English speakers, were the culprits. English, save as an abstraction, does not even exist, and certainly is not capable of taking action or making decisions. In fact, it might be argued that by moving the responsibility from English speakers to the English language, one lifts the burden of responsibility and guilt from the former, very real individuals, and places it on the latter, a meaningless abstraction, thus absolving those who are in fact guilty without penance.

This does not, of course, mean that either teaching or learning English is necessarily or intrinsically a bad thing. Rather, it merely emphasizes that in the process of teaching and learning *any* language, we need to be aware of the context in which the language is being taught and learned, the economic and power relationships present in that context that are related to the particular language, and the ideological power and status of the target language. We must also be aware of and concerned about the increasing tendency to commodify language—that is, treating a particular language as yet one more thing that an individual can possess. Learning English, for instance, does indeed open many doors—but at something of a price, at least if one is uncritical in accepting the language and the beliefs of its broader speaker community. This is true not only for English, but also for other languages, and especially for the small (and incredibly powerful) number of languages of wider communication (see, e.g., Calvet, 1999, 2002; Hagège, 1996).

The objectification of language leads not only to technicist approaches to language teaching, but also serves to reinforce ideologies of linguistic legitimacy. As I have suggested elsewhere,

> Underlying the educational discourse dealing with issues of language are a number of common assumptions about the nature of language, language structure, language difference, and so on, that tend to be shared by educators, parents, the general public, and indeed, by students themselves. Perhaps the most powerful of these assumptions concerns what counts as a "real" language, and, even more important, what does not count as a "real" language.... At issue here is what can be called linguistic legitimacy: which language varieties are deemed by the society to be legitimate, and which are not. (Reagan, 2002b, p. 60)

The idea that some language varieties are not legitimate is a powerful and dangerous one. It is an idea that periodically emerges, almost always in response to a perceived threat to the socially dominant language. Thus, we find African American English,[2] American Sign Language,[3] and various nonmainstream varieties of Spanish, French, and English all dismissed, from time to time, as somehow less than legitimate languages (see Reagan, 1997b, 2002b, pp. 57-82; Reagan & Osborn, 2002, pp. 33-54). Although the concept of linguistic legitimacy has no more credibility among linguists than does the idea that there are *primitive* languages, it is nevertheless an incredibly potent, and popular, idea among the general public, including many educators. By denigrating and delegitimizing an oppressed group's language, we in fact ensure that the group itself remains oppressed and dominated. It is here that the very real power of education to counter hegemonic forces may be most visible and powerful (see Andrews, 1998; Benesch, 2001; Canagarajah, 1999; Corson, 1999, 2001; Osborn, 2000; Pennycook 2001; Thomas & Wareing, 1999; Zamel & Spack, 2002).

TOWARD A SOLUTION: CRITICAL LANGUAGE STUDIES

If the objectification of language is as great a problem as has been suggested here, and if it is indeed as deeply embedded in our discourse as it would seem to be, then, to quote Lenin a bit out of context, "what is to be done?" The answer involves a return to our earlier discussion of positivism and positivistic epistemology. The positivistic approach to epistemology in general, and to the philosophy of science in particular, came under increasingly critical fire beginning in the early 1960s. The publication of

Thomas Kuhn's landmark work *The Structure of Scientific Revolutions* distinguished between periods of "normal science" and periods of "scientific revolution," and introduced the concept of paradigms and, even more powerfully, that of paradigm shifts, as important explanatory and conceptual elements to explain the difference between these two kinds of periods of scientific activity. A paradigm is far more than merely a model or a theory; as Patton explains,

> A paradigm is a world view, a general perspective, a way of breaking down the complexity of the real world. As such, paradigms are deeply embedded in the socialization of adherents and practitioners: paradigms tell them what is important, legitimate, and reasonable. Paradigms are also normative, telling the practitioner what to do without the necessity of long existential or epistemological consideration. But it is this aspect of paradigms that constitutes both their strength and their weakness—their strength in that it makes action possible, their weakness in that the very reason for action is hidden in the unquestioned assumptions of the paradigm. (1978, p. 203)

Thus, the dominant paradigm in a field of study at any given point in time essentially establishes the parameters within which legitimate discourse can take place. Kuhn explained the significance and power of the dominant paradigm in a field of study as follows:

> Scientists work from models acquired through education and through subsequent exposure to the literature often without quite knowing or needing to know what characteristics have given these models the status of community paradigms.... That scientists do not usually ask or debate what makes a particular problem or solution legitimate tempts us to suppose that, at least intuitively, they know the answer. But it may indicate that neither the question nor the answer is felt to be relevant to their research. Paradigms may be prior to, more binding, and more complete than any set of rules for research that could be unequivocally abstracted from them. (1962/1996, p. 46)

Kuhn's challenge to positivistic models of science was an important step in the articulation of more relativistic approaches to epistemology. Later philosophers of science expanded and extended Kuhn's critique (see, for example, Duerr, 1980, 1981; Feyerabend, 1987, 1991, 1993), while others have challenged at least the more radical approaches to epistemology advocated by some scholars (see D. C. Phillips, 2000). For our purposes here, the outcome of this ongoing philosophical debate is not particularly significant. What *is* significant is that there may be a paradigm shift on the horizon with respect to how we conceptualize and understand the construct of language.

Central to this paradigm shift with respect to how language is conceptualized are two related developments: first, the growing acceptance of constructivist models of teaching and learning in general (see Fosnot, 1996a, 1996b; Kaufman & Grennon Brooks, 1996; V. Richardson, 1997a), and in second/foreign language education in particular (see Reagan, 1999, 2002a; Reagan & Osborn, 2002, pp. 55-69; M. Williams & Burden, 1997), and second, the rise of critical and postmodern approaches to language education (see Benesch, 2001; Canagarajah, 1999; Fairclough, 1992; Osborn, 2003b; Pennycook, 2001). Both of these developments have been fairly widely addressed, but not in terms of their implications for challenges positivistic notions of language.

It is hard to imagine how we might exaggerate the role of language in human life. In a wonderful essay titled, "How to be the Centre of the Universe," Neil Smith has argued that:

> Language makes us human.... Whatever we do, language is central to our lives, and the use of language underpins the study of every other discipline. Understanding language gives us insight into ourselves and a tool for the investigation of the rest of the universe. Proposing marriage, opposing globalization, composing a speech, all require the use of language; to buy a meal or sell a car involves communication, which is made possible by language; to be without language—as an infant, a foreigner or a stroke victim—is to be at a devastating disadvantage. Martians and dolphins, bonobos and bees, may be just as intelligent, cute, adept at social organization and morally worthwhile, but they don't share our language, they don't speak "human." (2002, p. 3)

Assumptions and beliefs about language, as well as attitudes toward language, function in important ways to color and set the parameters of all social experience, and of educational experience in particular, and can, in the classroom and school contexts, serve either positive or negative ends (see Corson, 2001; Kubota, Austin, & Saito-Abbott, 2003; McKay & Hornberger, 1996; Osborn, 2003a; Reagan, 2001a, 2002b).

Critical language awareness actually constitutes a subset of language awareness, a concept that gained increasing popularity in the language education professions in the 1980s and 1990s. Language awareness has all of the characteristics of an educational slogan, and thus has been elusive with respect to any clear definition of its exact meaning. However, one reasonable attempt at defining the concept was made by a number of educational linguists in the early 1990s, and their working definition for the concept, which still seems reasonable, was that language awareness involved, "a person's sensitivity to and conscious awareness of the nature of language and its role in human life" (James & Garrett, 1992, p. 8). Such an awareness is certainly desirable and appropriate, but is also far from sufficient. As Norman Fairclough has suggested, *critical* language awareness is "an urgently needed element in language education [and] ... coming to be a prerequisite for effective democratic citizenship, and should therefore be seen as an *entitlement* for citizens, especially children developing towards citizenship in the educational system" (1992, p. 3, emphasis in original). Fairclough also notes that critical language awareness:

> presupposes and builds upon what is variously called "critical language study", "critical linguistics", or 'critical discourse analysis".... It also presupposes a critical conception of education and schooling.... It is vital first of all to situate both critical language study and [critical language awareness] in their social and historical contexts. (1992, p. 2)

And what is it that makes language awareness *critical*? Ultimately, language awareness is critical when one is concerned with the social, political, economic, historical, and ideological contexts in which language is used, and in which language must be metalinguistically and metacognitively understood (see Andrews, 1998; B. Johnson, 2003). In other words, critical language awareness involves the rejection of efforts and tendencies to objectify language and linguistic discourse. Beyond this, critical language awareness must also be understood to be not only an outgrowth of critical pedagogy (see Kanpol, 1994), but a necessary element of critical pedagogy in the second/foreign language context (see Janks, 1991, 1997; Janks & Ivanic, 1992; Osborn, 2000; Pennycook, 2000). As Catherine Wallace has suggested,

> A critical pedagogy presupposes an approach to language education in which learners and teachers aim to achieve some critical distance from language use in a range of spoken and written texts. Conversely, approaches under the broad umbrella of critical language awareness need to be located within a critical pedagogy if they are to have credibility as educational practice.... Critical understanding can be understood at two broad levels: first, in the cognitive sense of "conscious awareness"; secondly ... a deeper sense of "critical" as the ability and willingness to critique the ideological bases of language choice and variation. (1997, p. 241)

Critical language awareness, like critical pedagogy in general, is in the final analysis concerned with empowerment. Empowerment involves not only helping students to recognize, understand, and question discourse, but also, as Fairclough has pointed out, it "has a substantial 'shock' potential, and it can help people overcome their sense of impotence by showing them that existing orders of discourse are not immutable. The transformation of orders of discourse is a matter of the systemic de-structuring of existing orders and restructuring of new orders" (1989, p. 244). An important facet of this process of empowerment is recognizing that discourse is in fact *negotiated* between and among students and teachers. In short, as Karabel and Halsey observed in the late 1970s, "Teachers and pupils do not come together in a historical vacuum: the weight of precedent conditions the outcome of 'negotiation' over meaning at every turn" (1977, p. 58). Even the disempowered are not, after all, completely powerless. As Canagarajah has recently argued,

> If language learning is ideological ... the solution is not to run away from politics, but to negotiate with the agencies of power for personal and collective empowerment. If [English language teaching] is implicated in larger social processes and cultural practices, the corrective is not to eliminate that connection in favor of autonomy or "purity", but to seek a holistic pedagogy that will enable learners to engage with those domains for a richer educational experience. (1999, p. 197)

Why should language educators be concerned with being critical? Why, indeed, should *any* teacher be concerned with being critical in the sense in which the term is used in both critical pedagogy and critical language awareness? There are any number of ways in which these questions might be answered. We might, for instance, ground a response on the various codes of ethics that undergird the teaching profession (see Slattery & Rapp, 2003; Strike, Haller, & Soltis, 1988; Strike & Soltis, 1998). We might, alternately, base a response on the role, place of functions of schooling and education in a democratic society, with especial emphasis on the develop of meaningful critical thinking skills as a necessary preparation for the life of the citizen (see Apple & Beane, 1995; Gutmann, 1987; Soder, 1996; Stevens, Wood, & Sheehan, 2002). We could even try to address these questions by pointing out that the ability to generate a critical perspective is a key component of being an educated person—whether as a teacher, parent, citizen, or student. All of these are credible and valid responses, I believe, but perhaps the clearest and most forceful justification is that provided by Joan Wink for critical pedagogy in general:

> Why in the world does it matter? Kids matter. That's why. Our future matters. That's why. It is as simple as that. It is also something we all know. This is serious business we are talking about here. Students and teachers are hurting. We in education are a mirror of society that is more and more polarized. (2000, p. 165)

Precisely the same claims can be made for critical language awareness. Educators should be committed to encouraging the development of critical language awareness in our students because it is the right thing to do. It is a powerful way to promote social justice and the formation of a just, humane, and democratic society. It is also a way of helping individual children better understand the society in which they live, and better negotiate that society. It is, in essence, giving students the tools that they need to make their own decisions—and decisions not just about language, but about every aspect of human life. *This* is why we should be critical, and seek to promote the same in our students. Anything less is an abrogation of our duties as educators, as parents, as citizens, and as human beings. This does not, in any way, militate against the more common arguments that we use to defend the place of second/foreign language study in the general education curriculum; language skills are valuable for pragmatic, social, and cultural reasons as well as for political and ideological ones.

And this brings us back to our start, since in order to promote critical language awareness we are required to reject the positivist objectification of language, in favor of a more complex, sophisticated, and nuanced view of language. English does not exist, but *Englishes* do—and understanding this distinction is the key to developing a more critical, and cogent, view of language.

NOTES

1. Actually, this is precisely the sense in which Chomsky himself would likely deny that language exists—as Smith notes, Chomsky has argued that "there is no external reality" (Chomsky, 1993, p. 43), that "the question, 'to what does the word X refer?', has no clear sense," (Chomsky, 2000, p. 181) and finally, that relating linguistic mental representations to things in the world is not only not simple, but may be "perhaps even a misconceived project" (Chomsky, 1994, p. 159). See N. Smith (2002, pp. 100-104) for a detailed discussion of this point and of its implications.
2. There is a significant body of scholarly literature dealing with both the linguistic and the sociopolitical aspects of African American English. See, for example, Baugh (2000), Delpit and Dowdy (2002), Green (2002). McWhorter (1998), Mufwene, Rickford, Bailey, and Baugh (1998), and Rickford and Rickford (2000).
3. The linguistic literature that deals with American Sign Language is both extensive and theoretically sophisticated, and includes work addressing the structural features of American Sign Language (see Emmorey, 2003; Emmorey & Lane, 2000; Emmorey & Reilly, 1995; Liddell, 2003; Neidle, Kegl, Maclaughin, Bahan, & Lee, 2000; Valli & Lucas, 2000), the acquisition of American Sign Language as a first and second language (see Chamberlain, Morford, & Mayberry, 2000; Emmorey & Lane, 2000), the neurolinguistic and cognitive aspects of American Sign Language (see Emmorey, 2002; Emmorey & Lane, 2000), discourse and oral literature in American Sign Language (see C. Peters, 2000; Winston, 1999), the sociolinguistics of American Sign Language (see Lucas, 1995, 1996, 2001; Lucas,

Bayley, & Valli, 2001; Metzger, 2000), and comparative linguistics of different natural sign languages (see, for instance, Dively, Metzger, Taub, & Baer, 2001; Emmorey, 2003; Emmorey & Lane, 2000; Sutton-Spence & Woll, 1998). For discussions of the teaching and learning of American Sign Language as a second/foreign language, see Reagan (2000, 2002c) and Wilcox and Wilcox (1997).

CHAPTER 2

WHAT DOES IT MEAN TO KNOW A LANGUAGE?

Epistemological Reflections on Language Education

The traditional craft of the teacher can be rescued and strengthened by understanding the connection between the content area of the curriculum and how it will be understood by the student. Understanding this connection involves recognizing the cultural pattern of thought (the episteme*) that underlies the organization of knowledge in the curriculum unit as well as the phenomenological world of the student. The latter is essential for grasping what the student is likely to understand and how that understanding will be integrated into the student's pattern of thinking.*

—C. A. Bowers (1984, p. 78)

As a second/foreign language educator and linguist, I have often been asked how many languages I know. The question is well-intended and, for those who ask it, presumably reasonable. And yet, I have come to dread this question because providing an answer is so complex and difficult. The question assumes that *knowing* a language is pretty much an either-or matter; one either *knows* French or one doesn't. To a monolingual person, of course, such a dichotomy is both obvious and clear-cut; for the bilingual or multilingual individual, though, matters are a bit more uncertain.

Critical Questions, Critical Perspectives:
Language and the Second Language Educator, 17–33

What does it really mean to know a language? Is native competence what is required, or simply an ability to carry on a conversation in the language in a relatively fluent manner? Or are we, rather, concerned with knowledge *about* the language and its structure? For instance, I was once asked by a nonnative speaker of English to explain the second conditional; as a native speaker of English, I was completely at a loss, since I had no idea at all what the second conditional (or even the first conditional, for that matter) referred to.[1] In everyday speech, of course, *knowing* a language usually means being able to communicate in it rather than either native competence or knowing about the language, but even when used in this sense, there are problems. I can communicate in French relatively fluently in some contexts and about some topics, while in other contexts and with other topics, I may easily find myself struggling to understand and be understood. What does this say about my knowledge of French? Clearly, my knowledge is partial and incomplete—but then, do I, or do I not, know French?

One of the more significant challenges that faces us as second/foreign language educators is attempting to understand what, exactly, we mean by knowing a language. After all, underlying all pedagogical practice, ultimately, are questions of epistemology. The way in which we think about knowledge and what it means to know are directly and necessarily linked to all aspects of how we teach. In second/foreign language education, this can be seen clearly, for example, in the well-documented relationship between behaviorist learning theory and the audiolingual method (see Bernhardt, 1998; Chastain, 1976, pp. 109-129; Littlewood, 1984, pp. 17-21).

THE NATURE OF LEARNING THEORY

Traditionally part of philosophy, the attempt to understand what learning is really all about—and, concomitantly, how one might best encourage or support learning—has a long history, spanning thousands of years. Although the debate about learning precedes him, the ancient Greek philosopher Plato formulated a learning theory that remains credible today. In the *Meno,* Plato demonstrates how an uneducated slave boy could, through a process of guided questioning, seemingly produce an understanding of certain relatively sophisticated mathematical concepts. Plato's explanation for this was that since no *explicit* teaching of content took place, the knowledge demonstrated by the slave boy must have come from the boy. In other words, learning is essentially a matter of remembering or recalling what we already know (see, e.g., Cornforth, 1957; Grube, 1980; Nettleship, 1968). The Socratic teaching method, which involves active questioning by the teacher as well as continuous debate with students, is grounded in this idea. While obviously limited, such an approach to teaching does promote learning at least in those cases when knowledge and understanding can be gained deductively. More than this, though, the Platonic view of learning has a modern-day parallel that will be familiar to anyone interested specifically in language teaching and language learning. Noam Chomsky's conceptualization of universal grammar, coupled with the hypothetical "language acquisition device," is fundamentally a modern version of the Platonic view of learning, as applied to the case of language (see Cook & Newson, 1996, pp. 273-310). Children, as Steven Pinker has summarized the Chomskian position, "must be innately equipped with a plan common to the grammars of all languages, a Universal Grammar, that tells them how to distill the syntactic patterns out of the speech of their parents" (1994, p. 22). As Chomsky himself has explained,

> Even knowing very little of substance about linguistic universals, we can be quite sure that the possible variety of language is sharply limited.... The language each person acquires is a rich and complex construction hopelessly underdetermined by the fragmentary evidence available [to the child]. Nevertheless individuals in a speech community have developed essentially the same language. This fact can be explained only on the assumption that these individuals employ highly restrictive principles that guide the construction of grammar. (1975, pp.10-11)

Plato's view of learning was fundamentally speculative in nature, as were most of the learning theories that followed. The British philosopher John Locke, for instance, argued that the child's mind is essentially a tabula rasa—a blank slate, onto which the teacher may write whatever he or she thinks that the child should know (see Chambliss, 1987, pp. 71-85). Learning on such an account is, then, a matter of pouring knowledge into the child, rather than bringing knowledge out of the child. This Lockean perspective in turn served to support parts of nineteenth century psychology, which emphasized the different faculties of the mind and the need to furnish the mind with the best intellectual products of humanity (Tozer, Violas, & Senese, 1998, pp. 35-37). Nineteenth century psychology also contributed the idea that the mind can be best understood as a muscle, and that learning is thus comparable to exercise. Just as with exercise, learning is only meaningful and worthwhile if it is challenging. Coaches often remind their athletes that "no pain, no gain," and nineteenth century psychology advocated the training of the mind on the most challenging and difficult intellectual content—which was widely believed to be the study of the classical languages, and especially of Greek.

The development of psychology as a discipline distinct from philosophy led to an increasing emphasis on more scientific approaches to understanding human learning, and it is these nonspeculative approaches to learning that dominated the twentieth century (see Biehler & Snowman, 1990; Karier, 1986; Ormrod, 1995). Behaviorist learning theories obviously played a key role in education, perhaps nowhere more clearly than in the dominance of the audiolingual method in second/foreign language education for a good part of the twentieth century (see Richards & Rodgers, 2001, pp. 50-69).

What is especially intriguing in contemporary studies of learning is that although presented in the guise and rhetoric of scientific research, such theories remain in fact largely speculative in nature. Indeed, learning theories are not theories in a truly scientific sense at all—rather, they are metaphors that are used to try to represent, by analogy, what appears to be taking place as the individual engages in the learning process. The metaphors of Platonic and Lockean learning theories (i.e., pulling knowledge out of the student, and pouring knowledge into the student) are actually not all that different in kind from those of the behaviorists and other contemporary psychologists.

A recent publication of the National Research Council's Commission on Behavioral and Social Sciences in Education, titled *How People Learn: Brain, Mind, Experience and School*, begins with the assertion that:

> The revolution in the study of the mind that has occurred in the last three or four decades has important implications for education ... a new theory of learning is coming into focus that leads to very different approaches to the design of curriculum, teaching, and assessment than those often found in schools toda.... Thirty years ago, educators paid little attention to the work of cognitive scientists, and researchers in the nascent field of cognitive science worked far removed from classrooms. Today, cognitive researchers are spending more time working with teachers, testing and refining their theories in real classrooms where they can see how different settings and classroom interactions influence applications of their theories. (Bransford, Brown, & Cocking, 2002, p. 3)

Although I, too, am very interested in and excited by the developments in cognitive science, I have to say that I believe that the commission's enthusiasm is a bit premature. Cognitive science is indeed making fascinating discoveries about the human brain, and our knowledge of neuroscience is growing at a phenomenal rate (see Carter, 1998; Obler & Gjerlow, 1999; Purves et al., 1997; Solso, 1997; Thagard, 1996). Still, there is a huge chasm between what we know scientifically about the way in which the human brain functions and what the implications of this knowledge are for understanding individual learning, let alone for classroom practice.

We are beginning to develop powerful tools that allow us to observe the brain and brain activity in previously unimaginable ways, and such observations will almost certainly some day lead to scientifically-based learning theories. They have not done so yet, though, in spite of the plethora of books and articles purporting to apply brain research to the classroom (see, e.g., Jensen, 1998; Sylwester, 1995). In short, while a true science of learning is certainly possible, it has not yet emerged, nor is it likely to be articulated in pedagogically useful ways any time soon. We are, then, at least for the time being, reliant on metaphors to understand the nature of learning—one of the more powerful of which today is clearly constructivism.

There is a further point that is specific to second/foreign language education contexts that needs to be made here. In subject areas such as mathematics, biology, and history, we generally talk about students *learning* the subject matter. In language education, though, following the work of Stephen Krashen (see Dulay, Burt, & Krashen, 1982; Krashen, 1981, 1982, 1985), we have for a considerable period of time distinguished between *language learning* and *language acquisition*. While the distinction is both real and important, it is also the case, as Colin Baker has observed, that "the boundary between acquisition and learning is not distinct and separate" (2001, p. 87). Indeed, as we shall see in the following section of this chapter, with respect to constructivist approaches to epistemology, both language learning and language acquisition can be more than adequately explained and encouraged by constructivism and constructivist educational practices.

TOWARD AN UNDERSTANDING OF CONSTRUCTIVISM

Recently, a number of academic disciplines, led by scholars in mathematics, and followed by many working in the sciences, literacy, and language arts, have begun to undergo a significant change in the epistemological foundations which underlie their pedagogical practice (for science education, see, e.g., Fensham, Gunstone, & White, 1994; Mintzes, Wandersee & Novak, 1997; Tobin, 1993; for mathematics education, see, e.g., R. Davis, Maher & Noddings, 1990; Steffe, Cobb, & von Glasersfeld, 1988; T. Wood, Cobb, & Yackel, 1995; for literacy and language arts, see, e.g., Cooper, 1993; Kamii, Manning, & Manning, 1991; Nelson, 1996; Spivey, 1997). The change in epistemology that we are talking about is that of the growing popularity and credibility of constructivist approaches to learning theory.

Constructivism as an epistemology is, as we shall see, far from uniform, and is also far from new, dating back at least some 60 years to the work of

Jean Piaget (see Piaget, 1976, 1979, 1986, 1993, 1996), and, on at least some accounts, as far back as the work of eighteenth century German philosopher Immanuel Kant (see Boulter, 1997; Spivey, 1997, p. 6). Constructivism has, nonetheless, been relatively slow to impact significantly educational thought and practice in many areas, and is only now really beginning to come into its own in educational discourse (see Fosnot, 1996a; Grennon Brooks & Brooks, 1993). Although to some extent arguably implicit in many contemporary discussions about communicative language teaching, and while certainly quite relevant for second/foreign language practice, constructivist approaches to epistemology and learning theory have only recently, and relatively rarely, been explicitly examined in terms of their implications for second/foreign language teaching and learning (see Blyth, 1997; Craig, 1995; Kaufman & Grennon Brooks, 1996; Kumaravadivelu, 1994; Nyikos & Hashimoto, 1997; Reagan, 1999; Williams & Burden, 1997). In this chapter, an attempt will be made to encourage second/foreign language educators to consider seriously the potential contributions of constructivism to second/foreign language teaching and learning, first by providing a broad overview of the core assumptions and concepts of constructivism, and then by exploring the ways in which constructivism can inform and promote effective pedagogical practice in the second/foreign language context.

Although constructivism has gained considerable attention in the educational literature in recent years, there is no generally accepted consensus of what is actually meant by the term (see Duffy & Jonassen, 1992; Forman & Pufall, 1988; Kafai & Resnick, 1996; Nicaise & Barnes, 1996; Phillips, 1995, 1996; Schwandt, 1994; Steffe & Gale, 1995). As Virginia Richardson has noted, "One cannot think of constructivist teaching ... as a monolithic, agreed-upon concept.... There are fundamental theoretical differences in the various constructivist approaches" (1997b, p. 3). Indeed, there is even debate about whether constructivism is best understood as an epistemology, an educational philosophy, a pedagogical approach, a theory of teaching, or a theory of learning (see Kaufman & Grennon Brooks, 1996, p. 234). As Catherine Fosnot has observed,

> Constructivism is not a theory about teaching. It's a theory about knowledge and learning. Drawing on a synthesis of current work in cognitive psychology, philosophy, and anthropology, the theory defines knowledge as temporary, developmental, socially and culturally mediated, and thus, non-objective. Learning from this perspective is understood as a self-regulated process of resolving inner cognitive conflicts that often become apparent through concrete experience, collaborative discourse, and reflection. (Fosnot, 1993, p. vii)

Fosnot has further articulated this view, suggesting that:

> Constructivism is a theory about learning, not a description of teaching. No "cookbook teaching style" or pat set of instructional techniques can be abstracted from the theory and proposed as a constructivist approach to teaching. Some general principles of learning derived from constructivism may be helpful to keep in mind, however, as we rethink and reform our educational practices. (1996b, p. 29)

Such a view of constructivism essentially confirms its status as an epistemology—concerned with understanding and explaining knowledge and learning, rather than as an explicit theory of teaching (see von Glasersfeld, 1993, pp. 23-24). As an epistemology, constructivism entails the rejection of traditional transmission-oriented views of learning, as well as behaviorist models of learning. Instead, emphasis is placed on the individual learner's construction of his or her knowledge. Beyond this, constructivism assumes not only that learning is constructed, but also that the learning process is a personal and individual one, that learning is an active process, that learning is collaborative in nature, and that all learning is situated (see Merrill, 1992, p. 102). In other words, what constructivism offers is a radically different view of the nature of the learning process—a view that is grounded in a rejection of what von Glasersfeld has called the "domination of a mindless behaviorism" (1995a, p. 4). This view includes a number of general principles of learning, including:

- Learning is not the result of development; learning *is* development. It requires invention and self-organization on the part of the learner.
- Disequilibrium facilitates learning. *Errors* need to be perceived as a result of learners' conceptions and therefore not minimized or avoided.... Contradictions, in particular, need to be illuminated, explored, and discussed.
- Reflective abstraction is the driving force of learning. As meaning-makers, humans seek to organize and generalize across experiences in a representational form.
- Dialogue within a community engenders further thinking. The classroom needs to be seen as a "community of discourse engaged in activity, reflection, and conversation."
- Learning proceeds toward the development of structures. As learners struggle to make meaning, progressive structural shifts in perspective are constructed—in a sense, "big ideas."... These big ideas are learner-constructed, central organizing principles that can be generalized across experiences and that often require the undoing or reorganizing of earlier conceptions. This process continues throughout development (Fosnot, 1996b, pp. 29-30).

It is important to stress here that constructivist epistemology is more than simply an *alternative* to other epistemological approaches; rather, it entails a rejection of some of the core assumptions that have been shared by Western epistemology for some two and a half millennia (see Gergen, 1982, 1995). As von Glasersfeld has argued, "the crucial fact [in understanding constructivism is] that the constructivist theory of knowing breaks with the epistemological tradition in philosophy" (1995a, p. 6), which is why it has been labeled not merely postmodernist, but *post-epistemological* by some writers (see Noddings, 1990).

Thus far in this chapter, we have discussed constructivism as a single entity, although trying to keep in mind Richardson's warning that it is far from monolithic. It has become fairly commonplace in discussions of constructivism to distinguish between what are often taken to be two fundamentally distinct, competing *types* of constructivism (see Cobb, 1994, 1996; Magadla, 1996). The first type of constructivism, radical constructivism, is fundamentally an epistemological construct which has been most clearly and forcefully advocated in the work of Ernst von Glasersfeld (1984, 1989, 1993, 1995a, 1995b, 1996). Radical constructivism has its philosophical roots in Piaget's genetic epistemology (Piaget, 1979; Sinclair, Berthoud, Gerard, & Venesiano, 1985), and is essentially a cognitive view of learning in which "students actively construct their ways of knowing as they strive to be effective by restoring coherence to the worlds of their personal experience" (Cobb, 1996, p. 34). Radical constructivism is premised on the belief that an individual's knowledge can never be a *true* representation of reality (i.e., in an observer-independent sense), but is, rather, a construction of the world that s/he experiences. In other words, knowledge is not something that is passively received by the learner; it is, quite the contrary, the result of active mental work on the learner's part. From a radical constructivist perspective, knowledge is not something that can merely be conveyed from teacher to student, and any pedagogical approach that presumes otherwise must be rejected.

The alternative to radical constructivism is social constructivism, which has as its primary theoretical foundation the work of Vygotsky (1978, 1986; see also Moll, 1990). Social constructivism, while accepting the notion that the individual does indeed construct his or her own knowledge, argues that the process of knowledge construction inevitably takes place in a sociocultural context, and that therefore knowledge is in fact *socially* constructed. As Driver, Asoko, Leach, Mortimer, and Scott have argued with respect to science education, "it is important … to appreciate that scientific knowledge is both symbolic in nature and also socially negotiated.… The objects of science are not phenomena of nature but constructs that are advanced by the scientific community to interpret nature" (1994, p. 5).

The tension between radical and social constructivism, between the personal and the social construction of knowledge, although important philosophically, is in practice actually amenable to resolution (see, e.g., Cobern, 1993; Confrey, 1995). As Paul Cobb has asserted, "the sociocultural and cognitive constructivist perspectives each constitute the background for the other" (1996, p. 48), and von Glasersfeld has recognized that "we must generate an explanation of how 'others' and the 'society' in which we find ourselves living can be conceptually constructed on the basis of our subjective experiences" (1995a, p. 12). Perhaps the most reasonable way to articulate the common, shared elements of radical and social constructivism is to talk about learning as "socially mediated but personally constructed," a formulation which allows us to move away from the strong bifurcation of radical and social constructivism, and which also allows us to move on to a discussion of the implications of constructivist epistemology for teaching practice.

CONSTRUCTIVIST APPROACHES TO TEACHING

Constructivism is not, and cannot be conceptualized as, a pedagogical theory or approach per se, but certain characteristics of the constructivist-based classroom can be identified. For example, Grennon Brooks and Brooks (1993) and Kaufman and Grennon Brooks (1996) have identified eight characteristics that have been observed in constructivist classrooms:

- Use raw data and primary sources, along with manipulative, interactive, and physical materials.
- When framing tasks, use cognitive terminology, such as *classify, analyze, predict, create,* and so on.
- Allow student thinking to drive lessons. Shift instructional strategies or alter content based on student responses.
- Inquire about students' understandings of concepts before sharing your own understandings of those concepts.
- Ask open-ended questions of students and encourage students to ask questions of others.
- Seek elaboration of students' initial responses.
- Engage students in experiences that might engender contradictions to students' initial hypotheses and then encourage a discussion.
- Provide time for students to construct relationships and create metaphors. (Kaufman & Grennon Brooks, 1996, p. 235)

These characteristics function both as descriptive and normative attributes: they have been observed in practice, and can be (and have been) used for evaluation purposes. It is important to note here that, "[m]any of these attributes are not unique to constructivist teaching but are representative of good teaching in general" (Kaufman & Grennon Brooks, 1996, p. 235)—a point which would seem to confirm von Glasersfeld's claim that, "[c]onstructivism does not claim to have made earthshaking inventions in the area of education; it merely claims to provide a solid conceptual basis for some of the things that, until now, inspired teachers had to do without theoretical foundation" (1995a, p. 15). Furthermore, although it is true that "constructivist principles of learning do not automatically engender principles of teaching—[since] learners construct meaning on their own terms no matter what teachers do," (Winitzky & Kauchak, 1997, p. 62), it is also true that, "constructivist theorists would maintain—that learning is better or more effective when teachers use constructivist teaching methods, like culturing and keying bacteria as opposed to lecturing about bacteria. Constructivist teaching typically involves more student-centered, active learning experiences, more student-student and student-teacher interaction, and more work with concrete materials and in solving realistic problems.... Nevertheless, students still create their own meanings based on the interaction of their prior knowledge with instruction, and the meanings they make may not be the ones the teacher had in mind, no matter how constructivist the instruction.... Teachers create constructivist learning experiences for students based necessarily on what they, the teachers, find salient. But what is salient to the teacher is not necessarily so to the learner" (Winitzky & Kauchak, 1997, pp. 62-63). With this caveat in mind, we now turn to an examination of the implications of constructivist epistemology for second/foreign language education.

IMPLICATIONS OF CONSTRUCTIVIST EPISTEMOLOGY FOR SECOND/FOREIGN LANGUAGE EDUCATION

Constructivism has a wide range of implications for language educators, both in terms of its significance for research and its relevance for pedagogical practice. With respect to the former, studies of the social nature of language learning and acquisition are increasingly grounded in constructivist epistemological positions. Writing about developments in bilingual education, for instance, Christian Faltis has noted that "a shift toward the constructivist, social nature of learning and language acquisition is also increasingly evident in new research efforts" (1997, p. 194). Similarly, the veritable explosion in discourse studies is ultimately, albeit often implicitly, linked to constructivist approaches to understanding, whether one is concerned with academic discourse (see Achard, 1993; Bourdieu, Passeron & de Saint Martin, 1994), classroom discourse (see Bartolomé, 1998; Craig, 1995; Measures, Quell, & Wells, 1997; van Lier, 1996; Woods, 1996), or scientific discourse (see Boulter, 1997). Indeed, Gunnarsson has gone so far as to suggest that:

> The complexity of the construction of knowledge has been focused on by scholars dealing with scientific discourse. Proceeding from ideas within the social constructivist tradition, they have developed a methodology for the purpose of understanding how science is created through discourse ... the social construction of scientific facts [has been described] as an antagonistic struggle among scientists, leading to a deliberate diminishing of the results of others and a leveling up—to a generalized level—of one's own results. Scientific facts are regarded as mere works; rhetoric determines what become scientific facts. (1997, p. 111)

The implications of such a view of the nature and role of scientific discourse for the classroom are significant.

It is the growing recognition of the significance of the social construction of conceptual understanding in science that has coincided with the development of a suitable methodology for investigating social situations involving talk. Science is now often seen within science education research as intimately constructed, through discourse, within communities of knowers. The following themes in research and discourse in science teaching and learning arise from the synthesis of constructivism and sociolinguistic methodology and can be seen in the major work in progress:

- The *complexity* of classroom discourse which has complex interactions with the ways teachers teach, the resources they use and with the particular phenomenon of science being studied;
- *Communities* in science and science classrooms having characteristic discourse patterns;
- *Collaboration* in classroom settings allowing the authentic practice of science and the development of appropriate discourse; and
- *Critiques* of science, its methodology, its boundaries, its status, and its language as a cultural construct (Boulter, 1997, p. 242).

Such research foci emphasize, not surprisingly, the social construction of language and discourse, but there is room as well for concern with the personal or individual construction of language. One powerful way in which we can conceptualize the personal construction of language has to do with the linguistic notion of idiolects: "The unique characteristics of the language of an individual speaker are referred to as the speaker's *idiolect*. English may then be said to consist of 400,000,000 idiolects, or the number equal to the number of speakers of English" (Fromkin & Rodman, 1993, p. 276). In other words, a transmission-based view of language learning is simply incompatible with the final outcome of such learning, since each individual speaker (whether native or nonnative) in fact constructs his or her own understanding of the target language, which will, in turn, be modified and can be evaluated by comparison with other speakers of the language. This is not, of course, to minimize in any way the key role played by interaction in the process of language learning. As Katherine Nelson has noted,

> Competence in constructing and using culturally defined categories of entities (objects, events, properties, etc.) has been shown to involve a number of different linguistic components, including superordinate labels and the vocabulary of inclusive hierarchies. These verbal components can account for aspects of conceptual development previously held to be perceptually based (e.g., grouping along lines of shape similarity) or logically based (e.g., set relations). The verbal contributions to the development of cultural categories are integrated with experientially derived categories.... The coordination and integration processes involved in the assembling of cultural taxonomies ... exemplify the more general problem encountered during the preschool years of reconfiguring individual experientially based representations established independently of linguistic input to accommodate knowledge systems displayed in language. This reconfiguration cannot be accomplished through individual constructive processes alone, but requires implicit and explicit collaboration with knowledge bearers. (1996, p. 332)

Although Nelson's focus is on language acquisition in early childhood, the same general claim would apply to second/foreign language learning with respect to the complementary and interactive roles of the individual and the social construction of language. This brings us to the implications of constructivist epistemology for second/foreign language pedagogy.

In the context of the second/foreign language classroom, the application of constructivist epistemology would necessarily undergird virtually all classroom practice. As Williams and Burden have explained,

> The literature on language teaching provides comprehensive accounts of different language teaching methodologies and is rich with ideas and techniques for teaching a language. However, what has become increasingly clear to us is the fundamental importance to teachers of an understanding of what is involved in the process of learning to inform and underpin our teaching of the language. Teachers' own conceptions of what is meant by learning, and what affects learning will influence everything that they do in

> the classroom. At the same time, in order to make informed decisions in their day-to-day teaching, teachers need to be consciously aware of what their beliefs about learning and teaching are. (1997, pp. 1-2)

This is, as far as it goes, true not only of second/foreign language teaching, but of all teaching. To be sure, second/foreign language pedagogy does indeed have many common features with other sorts of teaching—but it is also distinct in some key ways. Successful second/foreign language learning entails far more for the learner than merely learning content and skills. Gardner has suggested that, "languages are unlike any other subject taught in a classroom in that they involve the acquisition of skills and behaviour patterns which are characteristic of another community" (1985, p. 146), while Crookall and Oxford argue that, "learning a second language is ultimately learning to be another social person" (1988, p. 136). It is this need for the learner to reconstruct one's personal identity that is at the heart of second/foreign language learning, and it is in this process of reconstruction, rather than merely in terms of learning vocabulary and grammatical forms, that constructivist epistemology may be most useful.

Williams and Burden, in an effort to summarize and consolidate the implications of constructivism for second/foreign language learning, have identified the following basic propositions that they believe to be essential for language teachers to understand:

- There is a difference between learning and education.
- Learners learn what is meaningful to them.
- Learners learn in ways that are meaningful to them.
- Learners learn better if they feel in control of what they are learning.
- Learning is closely linked to how people feel about themselves.
- Learning takes place in a social context through interaction with other people.
- What teachers do in the classroom will reflect their own beliefs and attitudes.
- There is a significant role for the teacher as mediator in the language classroom.
- Learning tasks represent an interface between teachers and learners.
- Learning is influenced by the situation in which it occurs (Williams & Burden, 1997, pp. 204-208)

One example of a constructivist approach to second/foreign language teaching is provided by a teacher in an introductory Spanish class whose lesson focuses on the use of the verb *gustar* to indicate likes and dislikes.[2] The class begins with the teacher presenting the following short passage in Spanish, in which *gustar* is used in a number of different ways:

> *A mí me gusta bailar, pero a Ana no le gusta bailar. A mi hermana le gustan las flores, pero a mi padre no le gustan. A mis hermanos les gusta la música americana. A mí me gustan todos los tipos de música. A Juan y a Diana les gusta hablar francés. A Kelly y a mí nos gusta hablar español. ¿Qué te gusta a ti?*

Utilizing pictures and dramatic techniques, the teacher ensures that the students understand the meaning of the passage, although they have yet to learn the specifics of the use of *gustar.* The teacher then begins to elicit class input using the basic forms of *Me gusta* + singular object (as in *Me gusta el vino*). After several students have produced correct forms of this type, the teacher then introduces a plural object (*Me gustan las flores*), and asks a student, *¿Te gustan las flores?* Using additional elicitation techniques, the teacher moves around the room, by this point alternating both the first and second person forms and the singular and plural forms, as well as gradually introducing negative forms (*No me gustan las flores*). Students are now encouraged to converse in pairs, in a round-robin fashion, asking questions and giving answers. The teacher provides input only as needed, generally using stress to indicate a student error and encourage student self-correction. During this activity, the teacher also introduces the *Me gusta* + infinitive form (*Me gusta bailar*), and then encourages students to use constructions of this type to indicate activities that they enjoy. At this point, the teacher might also introduce the third person form (*Le gusta el chocolate*) and have students discuss the likes and dislikes of other students in the class, based on the information obtained in the earlier part of the class. By the end of the class, students have begun to master the use of the verb *gustar*; additional practice and further development of the use of *gustar* will be needed, of course, but students should already be in a position to offer a reasonably accurate description of how *gustar* is used—and should be able to do so without ever having explicitly encountered a formal explanation of the grammatical rules involved. Similar approaches can be used to teach virtually any linguistic structure, semantic relationship or lexical item in the target language, as well as helping students to develop their own personal competence in (and hence construction of) the target language broadly conceived. In fact, I believe that a compelling case could be offered for the claim that the greater the difference between a particular structure or vocabulary item in the learner's mother tongue and the target language, the more appropriate and effective a constructivist approach to language learning may prove to be. This point is similar to that made recently by Widdowson:

> we now know much more than our predecessors about what makes language real for its users, and we know what learners have to do if they are to aspire to be foreign language users themselves. My main point is that this heightened understanding about language, communication, community, and social identity has also to be applied to the contexts of the classroom and the realities and identities of language learners. To do this is really only to recognize, as our predecessors have done, that what we are teaching is not language as experienced by its users but a *foreign* language which, as a subject, has to be designed for learners. (1998, p. 332)

Thus, *telling* students about the difference between the verbs *ser* and *estar* in Spanish (a distinction that is, in fact, rather more complex than generally suggested in second/foreign language classrooms in any case)[3] might well be less useful than simply having them employ the verbs and gradually come to know, in part as a result of teacher correction, when each is appropriate.

Another example in which we can see a constructivist approach to second/foreign language teaching is provided in a second year (or even more advanced) Russian course, after students have mastered some of the grammatical basics of the language and have a small but growing vocabulary. The teacher could revisit student understandings of the **ТЫ / ВЫ** distinction (analogous to the *tu/vous* distinction in French) by presenting students with Pushkin's short poem "Ты и Вы" in which this distinction is the central focus of a love poem. The poem, in translation, reads as follows:

> The empty *you* [**ВЫ**] by the warm *thou* [**ТЫ**]
> She, by a slip of the tongue, replaced
> And all happy daydreams
> Stirred up in the soul in love.
> Before her pensively I stand,
> To take my eyes off her I have not the strength;
> And I tell her: how nice of *you* [**ВЫ**]!
> And think: how I love *thee* [**ТЫ**]! (Arndt, 1972, pp. 222-223)

The typical student understanding of the **ТЫ / ВЫ** distinction is fairly simplistic, with students mastering the singular / plural distinction reasonably well but not really internalizing the significance of the informal/formal semantic relationship. This is, of course, understandable since the distinction is alien to English speakers. Pushkin's poem, however, *requires* that one understand this semantic relationship, and provides a tool which can be effectively utilized in a classroom setting to help students to construct a more meaningful and productive understanding of the distinction.

In both of the instances that have been discussed here, while explicit and directive teaching is certainly possible, the alternative of teacher modeling and individual student construction of the linguistic target has much to commend it.

WHAT CONSTRUCTIVISM IS *NOT*

At this point, a few words about what constructivism is *not,* and what it does *not* call for in terms of educational practice, are perhaps needed. Given its contemporary popularity, it is hardly surprising that constructivism has been not only widely discussed, but that it had also been widely misunderstood and misapplied. We have already seen that constructivism is best understood not as a theory of teaching, but as a theory of learning. While there may be more or less effective ways of teaching that encourage or discourage student learning on a constructivist account, it is important to understand that no pedagogical approach would be excluded by a commitment to constructivist epistemology. Indeed, not only is there no such thing as a constructivistic teaching theory, but in fact conceptually such a thing could not even exist. By its very nature, constructivism encourages an eclectic approach to classroom instruction. The idea that direct instruction or lecturing is incompatible with constructivist learning theory is simply untrue.

Furthermore, while constructivism is clearly student-centered in its focus, this does not mean that the content and skills to be learned must be determined by the student. Constructivism provides us with a way to conceptualize the process of student learning, and certainly requires active participation by the student in his or her learning. It also entails the recognition that the ultimate responsibility for learning is the student's, not the teacher's. The student, rather than the teacher, has the absolute veto on whether learning takes place. The particular content and skills to be learned, though, are not necessarily determined by the student at all. The identification of instructional and learning objectives clearly falls in the area of the teacher's responsibilities, though the student's acquiescence is also necessary.

Finally, it is important to understand that constructivism explains not only how students learn, but also explains how they mislearn: in other words, students construct knowledge, but they can also *mis*construct knowledge. Simply because a student has constructed knowledge in a particular way does not mean that the knowledge constructed is true. Constructivist epistemology, at least in its more moderate forms, does not entail epistemological relativism. The beginning student in a French class who says, "*Nous parlez français*" may well have constructed knowledge, but if so, has done so incorrectly. The fact of knowledge construction (or in this case, knowledge misconstruction) carries no significance for the determination of the accuracy of the knowledge constructed.

CONCLUSION

Constructivist epistemology has clear implications for classroom practice, the curricula, student evaluation, and, indeed, virtually all aspects of the teaching/learning process (see Henning, 1995; Zietsman, 1996). Although not explicitly discussed in this chapter, constructivist epistemology also has the potential to impact in significant ways the preparation of language educators (see Condon, Clyde, Kyle, & Hovda, 1993; Osborn, 2004; Rainer & Guyton, 1994; V. Richardson, 1997a) and the challenge of preparing such educators to engage in reflective and analytic classroom practice (see Norlander-Case, Reagan, & Case, 1999; Parker, 1997; Reagan, Case, & Brubacher, 2000; Richards & Lockhart, 1994; Zeichner & Liston, 1996). The ultimate purpose of taking constructivist epistemology seriously in second/foreign language education, though, is to help teachers to learn to empower students to acquire language more effectively.

NOTES

1. For readers who share my puzzlement, the first conditional involves the form *If + present simple + will* (as in, "If I don't go to class, I won't pass the exam"), while the second conditional involves the form *If + past simple + would* (as in, "If I could do the work, I would pass"). The difference between the first and second conditional has to do with the probability of the hypothetical event; the first conditional refers to a situation that is both real and possible, while the second conditional involves situations that are unlikely to occur.
2. I am grateful to Jamie Bernetich for sharing this lesson (*Las cosas que nos gustan*) with me.
3. For instance, it is commonly taught that *estar* is used to describe a characteristic that is not inherent (as in *Estoy cansado*). As a generalized rule, this works reasonably well, but one is then faced with trying to explain why *muerto* (dead) (as in *Está muerto*) requires *estar* but *feliz/desgraciado* (happy/unhappy) require *ser* (as in *Soy feliz*), and so on. For a fairly typical example of the way in which the *estar/ser* distinction is presented in beginning Spanish textbooks, see Schmitt and Woodford (1997, pp. 278-282.)

CHAPTER 3

WHY STUDY A SECOND/ FOREIGN LANGUAGE?

Articulating Alternative Justifications for Language Study

One can, for instance, not see why millions of people, in the course of the years, have to learn two or three foreign languages which thereafter only a fraction of which they can use and which therefore the majority of them forget again completely, for out of a hundred thousand pupils who, for instance, learn French, hardly two thousand will later on be able to use it actually, while ninety-eight thousand, throughout their entire future course of life, will no longer be in a situation where they can make use of what they have learned.... Thus for the sake of two thousand people for whom the knowledge of this language is of use, actually ninety-eight thousand have to be tortured in vain and sacrifice valuable time.

—*Adolf Hitler* (1940, p. 627)

Adolf Hitler was certainly not alone in his rather hostile view of the teaching and learning of second/foreign languages. Indeed, in recent years advocating that all students ought to study a language other than their own has become, in most Anglophone settings, an increasing quixotic crusade to put it mildly.[1] Although perhaps understandable, this also consti-

Critical Questions, Critical Perspectives:
Language and the Second Language Educator, 35–43

tutes what may be the latest stage in a process of dramatic change in the status of languages and language learning in educational contexts in general. As Leo van Lier has noted,

> There was a time, from the ancient Greeks to the late Middle Ages, when language was central in educational practices, in the form of the three branches of the *trivium:* grammar, logic, and rhetoric. Then, increasingly, language study became separated from other subjects ... and became merely one other subject.... As a result, language lost its centrality and relevance as an educational focal point, and it became difficult to see how it connected to other parts of the curriculum. (1995, pp. 7-8)

There can be little doubt that the centrality of language study that once dominated education has been largely lost. In addition, many of the arguments that language educators have traditionally offered for the study of languages have increasingly come to be seen as irrelevant, misleading or even wrong-headed by students, parents, and even by many of our colleagues in other disciplines (see, e.g., Elvin, 1977, pp. 37-45). The dominance of English in the worlds of politics, commerce, pop culture, and scholarship[2] has meant that monolingual English speakers are increasingly secure and complacent in their monolingualism, and an ability to function in a second/foreign language for native speakers of English is less and less seen as the mark, let alone as a necessary condition, for being an educated person.[3]

In the U.S. context, second/foreign language education is at a critical point in its history.[4] Of course, this statement is a relatively safe one to make, since it largely describes the state of education as a field for as long as it has been a field (see, e.g., Herman, 2002; Schulz, 1988; Watzke, 2003). Enrollments in second/foreign language programs, on the whole, are at least stable, and there have been significant increases in both the numbers of students and the number of programs in public school settings (Rhodes & Branaman, 1999). In the post-9/11 world, there is also a growing concern about the shortage of competent second/foreign language professionals in U.S. society (see Wallinger, 2002). The teaching of languages is arguably of higher quality than has ever been the case (see, e.g., Grove, 2003; Lomas & Osoro, 1993; Watzke, 2003, pp. 99-131), as is the preparation of most second/foreign language educators, and the national standards developed by the American Council on the Teaching of Foreign Languages and its sister organizations are among the best articulated and conceptually well-grounded of any subject (see Lafayette, 1996; J. Phillips & Terry, 1999). At the same time, while enrollments in Spanish are growing dramatically, enrollments in many other commonly-taught languages (generally, French, German, and Latin) continue to decline or, at best, remain static. Indeed, on some accounts, German is even at risk of becoming something of a "less commonly taught language"[5] in the U.S. context—recent figures, for instance, show that German is offered in only 5% of U.S. elementary schools (compared with Spanish at 79%, French at 27%, and Japanese at 3%), and in only 24% of secondary schools (again, trailing Spanish, with 93%, and French, with 64%) (see Rhodes & Branaman, 1999, pp.16, 19; see also Watzke, 2003, pp. 181-186). Large numbers of U.S. students still do not study any second/foreign language at all, and, as Dell Hymes has noted, there continues to be a widely held but generally unarticulated view in the United States that everyone in the world worth speaking to speaks English, and that real bilingualism or multilingualism is probably unnatural and perhaps even harmful (1996, pp. 84-85).

In a way, all of this is reminiscent of the opening of Woody Allen's "Speech to the Graduates," in which he notes that, "more than any other time in history, mankind faces a crossroads. One path leads to despair and utter hopelessness. The other, to total extinction. Let us pray that we have the wisdom to choose correctly" (1980, p. 81). I believe that our choices today are somewhat more positive that those laid out by Allen, but I am also concerned that language education continues to be marginalized in the broader context of public education. Like truth, justice, and peace, second/foreign language education tends to be considerably more popular with the general public as a theoretical or principled construct than it is as a practical reality when funding is limited, as it inevitably is in the real world of educational institutions. The situation of language education in the United States is in many ways parallel to the status of the Irish language in contemporary Ireland. The sociolinguist Suzanne Romaine quotes one Irish interviewee as saying that, "although we are all *for* Irish as we are for cheaper bus fares, heaven and the good life, nobody of the masses is willing to make the effort" to learn and use the language (quoted in Romaine, 2000, p. 43). So, too, are most people in favor of language learning—a good thing so long as it does not raise taxes or interfere with the *real* job of education (see Osborn, 2000; Osborn & Reagan, 1998; Reagan, 2002a; Reagan & Osborn, 1998, 2002).

TRADITIONAL ARGUMENTS FOR SECOND/FOREIGN LANGUAGE STUDY

A significant part of the challenge that language educators face in making the case for the value of studying languages has been that our past arguments have sometimes tended to be a bit disingenuous. For instance, Gil Jarvis once argued, with respect to secondary students, that, "with a language skill added to your other skills, you might double the chances of getting the job you want. There are openings for an auto mechanic who also speaks Arabic, an electronic radio expert who knows Japanese.... Language is, in fact, your hidden job insurance" (1980, pp. 31-32). Now, while competence in a second/foreign language is an incredibly valuable skill, and although language skills do have very real vocational value, it is nevertheless a bit much to suggest that high school study of Arabic or Japanese, at least as they are currently taught in secondary schools in the United States (as well as in those relatively few schools in which they are offered at all), will prepare one to function in that language as an auto mechanic or electronics expert—even if the student had the necessary technical background skills and knowledge in English. At best, language study of one of these languages might provide one with the necessary linguistic skills to communicate at the most basic level (greetings, etc.) with customers—far from the kind of competence suggested by Jarvis. We sometimes have, in short, something of a truth-in-advertising problem about the benefits of second/foreign language study. The value of knowing a second/foreign language very well is quite different from the value of studying a second/foreign language, even for a few years. This distinction, obvious to most students, is one that has often been absent in the defenses we have offered for requiring language study. For the most part, advocacy of language study has tended to conflate the advantages of *knowing* a second/foreign language (that is, the advantages of *bilingualism*) with those associated with *studying* a second/foreign language (see Brèe, 1984; Brown, 1995; Met & Galloway, 1992). This is an important difference, since most people in Anglophone settings have direct experience only with the latter—and all too often, these experiences have been both frustrating and largely unsuccessful. The nineteenth century American humorist Mark Twain commented extensively on his own problems learning (or, perhaps more accurately, *not* learning) both German and French (see U. Thomas, 1988). In an essay on "Taming the Bicycle," Twain noted that:

> It [learning to ride a bicycle] is not like studying German, where you mull along, in a groping, uncertain way, for thirty years; and at last, just as you think you've got it, they spring the subjunctive on you, and there you are. No—I see now, plainly enough, that the great pity about the German language is, that you can't fall off it and hurt yourself. (Quoted in Loeb, 1996, p. 35)

In *The Innocents Abroad,* Twain discussed the problems of communicating with native speakers in French, observing, as perhaps have many others, that, "in Paris they just simply opened their eyes and stared when we spoke to them in French! We never did succeed in making those idiots understand their own language" (1869/1966, p. 484).

This does not mean, though, that there are not very strong and compelling arguments in favor of language study. These arguments, however, are in fact different from those we have traditionally offered, and focus on the benefits of language *study* itself, rather than on those of language *knowledge*. Let me suggest that there are at least three sets of reasons for encouraging students to study languages other than their own: epistemological arguments, sociopolitical arguments, and interpersonal arguments. These arguments are significantly different from those in favor of bilingualism. There can be no doubt that for those who achieve competence in a second/foreign language, the benefits of such competence are considerable. But, as I have already suggested, for many—indeed, for the majority—of our students, such competence is an unlikely outcome of second/foreign language study. It is for this reason that the arguments in favor of language *study* itself become so important.

EPISTEMOLOGICAL ARGUMENTS FOR SECOND/FOREIGN LANGUAGE STUDY

One of the reasons for studying a variety of disciplines, as in the tradition of *general education* as the foundation for the liberal arts, is that each discipline approaches problems in its own unique manner. Thus, by studying history students learn something about the way in which historians think, just as by studying biology, they learn how biologists think. To be sure, initial and limited study in a particular discipline does not mean that students master the epistemological approaches used in the discipline—that comes only with in-depth, long-term study—but the basic idea in the liberal arts is that they should come away from the experience with at least a clearer understanding of how each discipline organizes the world. Study of language can contribute to this understanding on two levels. First, the formal study of a language provides students with a metalanguage for discussing the characteristics and components of any language, including their native language. For instance, it is not unusual for an individual to claim that they never really understood *grammar* and grammatical relations until they studied a second/foreign language. To some extent, of course, this only makes sense—one does not really need a formal, articulated understanding of the grammar of one's own language in order to function in the language. Second, and perhaps more important, the study of language can be more fundamental epistemologically than the study of any other discipline, since different languages do indeed construct reality in somewhat different ways (see Reagan, 1999; Williams & Burden, 1997). Although linguistic relativism remains a somewhat controversial topic,[6] there is growing acceptance among linguists that at least in a weak form, the idea that "human perceptions of reality are structured and constrained—not controlled, but structured and constrained—by human languages, in interesting and significant ways" (Elgin, 2000, p. 52), is absolutely correct. Further, as the philosopher Michel Foucault has argued, even the effort to "name" things is, ultimately, about issues of power, control, and, ultimately, violence (see S. Ball, 1990; Foucault, 1970, 1972, 1973 1975; Merquior, 1985). In other words, language can and does play an important role in how we perceive and understand reality, and recognition of this role of human language can be an important outcome of the study of *any* language.

SOCIOPOLITICAL ARGUMENTS FOR SECOND/FOREIGN LANGUAGE STUDY

The sociopolitical arguments for language study, especially for native speakers of English, are important because they focus on raising the language awareness of students (see Andrews, 1998; Benesch, 2001; Fairclough, 1992). In essence, the sociopolitical arguments are concerned with helping students to understand issues of power, domination, and subordination related to language, language use, language status, language variation, and language attitudes. Although such understanding can come in a monolingual context, as in the case of the explicit study of the use of academic discourse (see Bartolomé, 1998; Bourdieu, Passeron, & de Saint Martin, 1994), it is both more powerful and clearer when explored in a bi- or multilingual context, as can and should be the case in the second/foreign language classroom. It is just such a concern, incidentally, which underlies the work of Michel Foucault; as one German commentator has noted,

> The focus of Foucault's investigation is "power". It is his conviction that power is the principle of development and integration within society. If this premise is accepted as a general rule, then power as a practical principle must also apply as a principle for a theoretical system of knowledge. In fact, power and knowledge are the main themes of Foucault's work.... The changing order of knowledge and power is historically conditioned and our lack of knowledge of these conditions leads us to believe that our present state of existence is the *epitomé* of humanity. Historical and philosophical reflection upon the past reveals that the anthropological generalizations that arise in the course of our daily lives are illusions.... The theoretical disciplines that reflection incorporates are *genealogy*—the theory of power practices—and *archeology*—the theory of discourse and knowledge. (Fink-Eitel, 1988, pp. 1-2)

While the epistemological arguments for language study emphasize the ways in which different languages construct reality, the sociopolitical arguments, in short, emphasize the impact of reality (in political and power-related terms) on language and language use. In essence, the sociopolitical arguments in favor of language study are concerned with helping students to appreciate the social contexts of language use, especially with respect to the roles played by language and language use in establishing and maintaining differential power relations in society (see Reagan & Osborn, 1998; Thomas & Wareing, 1999). As Lourdes Ortega has noted, one of the challenges in the field of second/foreign language education has been its failure "to recognize the fact that both societal attitudes towards languages and power struggles resulting from ownership of a language and a culture by particular groups are inextricably embedded in the definition of goals for language education" (1999, p. 243). The sociopolitical arguments for language study require that as language educators we incorporate not simply concern with the teaching and learning of languages in our profession, but also concerns with issues of social justice both broadly conceived and in the specific context of the language classroom (see Corson, 1999, pp. 6-27; Ehrenreich, 2003; Kubota, Austin & Saito-Abbott, 2003; Osborn, 2000; Osborn & Reagan, 1998). Finally, an important element of the sociopolitical arguments for language study is that such study is a valuable tool in helping students to understand the symbiotic negotiation that takes place between language and reality.

INTERPERSONAL ARGUMENTS FOR SECOND/FOREIGN LANGUAGE STUDY

In any communicative interaction where one person is speaking his or her native language, and the other is using that language as a second or additional language (fairly typical of the linguistic encounters of native speakers of English with speakers of other languages), the former have a huge advantage over the latter (see Ammon, 2003). This fundamental inequity in the linguistic interactions between native and nonnative speakers is both powerful and problematic. As David Jordan has commented, "if [a language] is unequally known, as between native and non-native speakers, the negotiation [of meaning] is not 'fair.'... Linguistic competence becomes a political resource; leadership falls to the better speakers" (1997, p. 39). In fact, it has been the concern with such inequality of power between native and nonnative speakers that has in part motivated advocates of international auxiliary languages such as Esperanto (see Janton, 1993; Nuessel, 2000), although, as Jane Edwards as perceptively noted, "the fact is, that, given the nature of the Esperanto movement, excellent Esperanto is one of the modes of establishing oneself as a person of importance in the movement.... In fact, generally speaking, the qualifications for leadership in the Esperanto movement are good Esperanto, a willingness to work for the propagation of the language, and to have no outward signs of being certifiably insane" (1993, p. 29). In other words, differential linguistic and communicative ability in the second/foreign language seems inevitably to result in differences both in terms of perceptions of competence and with respect to real differences in situational power and control. Perhaps among the clearest examples of such differences in power, status, and control can be found in the context of the teaching of English to speakers of other languages internationally, where the distinction between teachers who are *native speakers* and those who are *nonnative speakers* is often an incredibly important one (see Brutt-Griffler & Samimy, 1999; Liu, 1999). To be sure, this type of linguistic inequity is by no means necessarily eliminated or even reduced by second/foreign language study, but the process of language study may at least make a contribution to helping the native speaker become more aware of and sensitive to his or her dominance of the communicative situation.

CONCLUSION

In conclusion, I believe that language study can be immensely valuable, but I also believe that language educators have relied on arguments and defenses of second/foreign language study that confuse the benefits of language *knowledge* with those of language *study*. What I have attempted to accomplish in this chapter is to lay out, admittedly in a very brief manner, some alternative arguments that might be used for advocating language study as part of the more general education of the university student. These arguments are not intended, of course, to replace the very real and powerful arguments for the need for true language proficiency, but rather, to provide support for those arguments, especially given the large number of cases where language students will never really achieve proficiency.

NOTES

1. My focus in this chapter is on higher education in Anglophone contexts in general, and the U.S. case in particular. Clearly, the situation is somewhat different in societies in which English is not the vernacular language. In such settings (which include the vast majority of the world, of course) the arguments for studying and learning a second/foreign language (and especially for studying and learning English) are often both more powerful and

successful. This is the case even when the vernacular language is also a "language of wider communication" such as French or Spanish.

2. The dominance of English in the world has been a matter of considerable interest and concern to linguists, educators and policymakers, and there is an extensive literature available detailing the nature, origins, and likely outcomes of linguistic imperialism and English dominance. See, for instance, Brutt-Griffler (2002), Crystal (2003), Durand (2001), Graddol (1998), Hagège (2000), Hall and Eggington (2000), Pennycook (1994, 1998), Phillipson (1992, 2003), and Tonkin and Reagan (2003).
3. What constitutes an educated person is obviously socially determined, and varies from time and place. There is a rich philosophical literature dealing explicitly with questions of education and the educated person; see, for instance, the extensive work of R. S. Peters (1967, 1973) and Hirst (1974) on these topics (see also Dearden, Hirst & Peters, 1972; Hirst & Peters, 1970; Noddings, 1995).
4. It is important to note that the focus of this chapter is on second and additional language learning for native speakers of English; the situation with respect to native speakers of languages other than English in the U.S. context is quite different and distinct (see Campbell & Rosenthal, 2000; Ovando & Gourd, 1996).
5. The phrase *less commonly taught language* is used in the U.S. context to refer to languages other than French, Latin, Spanish, and, traditionally, German. Although common, the phrase is in fact something of a catch-all category, and a problematic one at that (see Reagan, 2002d; Reagan & Vorster, 2000). See Chapter 5 for a more in-depth discussion of the less commonly taught languages.
6. See Lee (1996) for an excellent discussion of the linguistic relativity hypothesis.

CHAPTER 4

WHO DECIDES WHICH LANGUAGE?

Power and Language Rights in Education

The Second World War involved violations of human rights on an unprecedented scale but its ending saw the dawn of a new era for rights. Following their heyday in the seventeenth century ... rights played a crucial role in the revolutions of the late eighteenth century. In the nineteenth and early twentieth centuries, however, appeal to rights was eclipsed by movements such as utilitarianism and Marxism which could not, or would not, accommodate them.... The contemporary period has seen a further shift in their fortunes and today they provide an accepted international currency for moral and political debate. In many parts of the world, irrespective of cultural or religious traditions, when issues or torture or terrorism, poverty or power are debated, the argument is very often conducted in terms of rights and their violation.

—*Brenda Almond* (1993, p. 259)

The past century has seen not only challenges to and abrogations of human rights, but also a growing awareness and articulation of such rights. One area in which such awareness has been relatively late to develop, in spite of ongoing and often egregious violations of group and individual rights, is that of language. As recently as 1985, Gomes de

Critical Questions, Critical Perspectives:
Language and the Second Language Educator, 45–58

Matos could write that, "Although ours has been said to be 'the age of rights' ... there has not yet been a thorough, well-documented, carefully thought out discussion of the crucial problem of the human being's linguistic rights" (1985, pp. 1-2). Given the centrality of language to self-identification and to our sense of who we are, and where we fit in the broader world, it is interesting that a concern with language rights has taken so long to emerge. And yet, such concern *has* emerged in recent decades, and the scholarly and political literature dealing with issues of language rights has increased dramatically both quantitatively and qualitatively (see, i.e., Herriman & Burnaby, 1996; Kontra, Phillipson, Skutnabb-Kangas & Várady, 1999; Phillipson, 2000; Skutnabb-Kangas & Phillipson, 1995). Although it is clear that we have a long way to go in terms of raising consciousness about language rights, and while such rights are far from universally recognized (let alone universally observed or enforced), the fact that the issue itself has been put on the table for discussion and debate is itself promising.

In this chapter, I want to present an overview of the concept of language rights as a special type of human rights, especially with respect to the implications of the concept of language rights for language policy in the educational sphere. We will then turn to an examination of the place and violation of language rights in the context of contemporary public education in the United States.

TOWARD A DEFINITION OF LANGUAGE RIGHTS

The fundamental challenge presented by debates about language and language policy is essentially that of achieving balance between the competing goods of social unity and access on the one hand, and respect for and toleration of diversity on the other (see R. Cooper, 1989; Kaplan & Baldauf, 1997; Tollefson, 1991). Basically, the question that policymakers are trying to address in such debates is the extent to which pluralism, as a necessary condition for a democratic social order, applies to the issue of language. At the heart of this discussion, of course, is the issue of language rights. In other words, to what extent, and in what ways, are *language* rights *human* rights? Also relevant here is the related question of whether rights (in this case, language rights) apply only to the individual, or whether there are rights which are group rights (that is, which apply to a community rather than solely to the members of that community by virtue of some common, shared feature of the individuals in the community) (see Coulombe, 1993; Tollefson, 1991, pp. 167-200). This is actually a far more complex matter than it might at first seem, since language rights are "preeminently *social,* in that they are only comprehensible in relation to a group of other human beings with whom the language is shared and from which personal and cultural identity is achieved" (MacMillan, 1982, p. 420). In other words, debates about language rights are unique in that, as Kenneth McRae has argued, "societies characterized by linguistic pluralism differ from those characterized by racial, religious, class or ideological divisions in one essential respect, which stems from the pervasive nature of language as a general vehicle of communication" (1978, p. 331). This having been said, the concept of group rights is itself somewhat problematic, potentially leading to an apartheid-style mandate of ethnic obligation, even as the alternative of linguistic imperialism looms large (see Pennycook, 1994; Phillipson, 1992). The challenge, in short, is a very real one, with very real outcomes.

In working toward a conception of language rights, a good place to begin our discussion is with the United Nation's Declaration on the Rights of Persons Belonging to National or Ethnic, Religious and Linguistic Minorities (adopted December 18, 1992), in which the international community attempted to articulate the nature of the human and civil rights which ought to be accorded members of minority groups. This declaration was a follow-up to the Universal Declaration of Human Rights, necessitated by the widespread violation of the second article of the Universal Declaration of Human Rights which prohibits discrimination against individuals based on language. Specifically, three articles of the declaration are relevant for our purposes here. First, Article 2.1 prohibits what might be termed active discrimination against members of minority groups:

> Persons belonging to national or ethnic, religious and linguistic minorities (hereinafter referred to as persons belonging to minorities) have the right to enjoy their own culture, to profess and practice their own religion, *and to use their own language, in private and in public, freely and without interference or any form of discrimination.* (Article 2.1, my emphasis)

This, in a sense, is the negative force of the declaration, in that it focuses on simply prohibiting actions and policies that unfairly target minority groups. The declaration goes far beyond this negative constraint, however, and in Articles 4.2 and 4.3 specifies what can be called positive, or proactive, language rights:

> States shall take measures to create favorable conditions to enable persons belonging to minorities to express their characteristics and to develop their culture, language, religion, traditions and customs, except where specific practices are in violation of national and contrary to international standards. (Article 4.2)

> States should take appropriate measures so that, whenever possible, persons belonging to minorities have adequate opportunities to learn their mother tongue or to have instruction in their mother tongue. (Article 4.3)

These explicit statements of both negative and positive aspects of language rights differ in significant ways, of course, from the legal and constitutional provisions governing the issue of language rights in the vast majority of member states of the United Nations, including, notably, the United States. Even more important in this context, though, are the very common gaps between legal and constitutional protections and the reality of daily life in societies around the world. Constitutional guarantees are certainly desirable, but they are by no means *sufficient* to ensure justice.

Violations of language rights occur in a wide variety of contexts and settings, and take many forms. Underlying many violations of language rights are assumptions tied to ideologies of linguistic imperialism (Pennycook, 1995). Linguistic imperialism is not language-specific; virtually any linguistic community *could* utilize its language to dominate others and to promote linguistic hegemony. In the real world, though, few language communities have the political, economic, cultural, and military power and status to engage in such linguistic imperialism. The role of English in the contemporary world is often cited as the clearest example of linguistic imperialism. Robert Phillipson, for instance, has provided a compelling critique of English linguistic imperialism, arguing that it is characterized by situations in which "*the dominance of English is asserted and maintained by the establishment and continuous reconstitution of structural and cultural inequalities between English and other languages*" (1992, p. 47, emphasis in original). I think that there can be little doubt about the increasing dominance of English in the international sphere (see, for instance, Crystal, 2003; McArthur, 1998), and in fact it is the very success of English that makes it such a danger and threat to many smaller languages. However, English is by no means alone; the same sort of linguistic imperialism also colors the relations between French and indigenous languages in many parts of the world, between Spanish and Amerind languages in Latin America, and, of course, at least historically, characterized the relationship between Russian and the other languages of the former Soviet Union and the Soviet bloc.

The desire for a common language for intercommunication is not itself evidence for linguistic imperialism, of course. Linguistic imperialism goes beyond such needs, either explicitly or implicitly encouraging linguistic assimilation to the dominant language, and involving a complex set of attitudes and beliefs about language and the contexts in which particular languages are functional. In other words, linguistic imperialism has at its core the exploitation of dominated language communities in favor of the dominant language community. The selection of a language for use in any given setting is associated with a number of factors, but whether the communicative situation is an informal one between two individuals or a matter of government policy, the selection of a language to be used is, in any context where bi- or multilingualism exists, at least in part a *political* choice.

Related to linguistic imperialism is a broader kind of social and ideological bias, which has come to be called linguicism. Linguicism is essentially the linguistic aspect of racism, sexism, ageism, and so on; the term refers to "ideologies, structures, and practices which are used to legitimate, effectuate, and reproduce an unequal division of power and resources (both material and immaterial) between groups which are defined on the basis of language" (Phillipson, 1992, p. 47). Among the manifestations of linguicism are claims about linguistic legitimacy: that is, debates about what counts as a language (see Reagan, 1997b). Debates about linguistic legitimacy are virtually always reflective of differential power relations; one does not come across arguments about whether French or German are legitimate languages, but one *does* find otherwise reasonable people suggesting that signed languages, artificially constructed languages such as Esperanto, and nonmainstream language varieties should not be treated as *real* or *legitimate* languages.

The effects of linguistic imperialism and linguicism at their most extreme can be seen in the growing number of languages whose very existence is threatened (see Dorian, 1998). Grenoble and Whaley, for instance, have argued that:

> Over the course of the next century ... a certain small group of languages (Arabic, Chinese, English, and Spanish, to name a few) will be used by an ever increasing percentage of the world's population, while a great many other languages will completely disappear. Just how many will disappear is a matter open to debate, though according to the more dire predictions of Michael Krauss, over 4,000 of the world's languages will cease to be spoken by the end of the century. (1998a, p. viii)

Some scholars, most notably Tove Skutnabb-Kangas, have suggested that what is actually taking place in many instances is not merely language death, but is in fact linguistic genocide (see Skutnabb-Kangas, 2000). This is a very strong claim, of course, but one for which the evidence in many cases is quite powerful (see, e.g., Bobaljik, Pensalfini, & Storto, 1996; Hernández-Chávez, 1995; Hindley, 1990; Skutnabb-Kangas & Bucak, 1995).

It is important to note here that while the relatively small number of languages of wider communication, and English in particular, are most often identified as the dominating and even oppressing languages in conflicts between language groups, the tables can be quickly turned. As John Edwards has observed,

> It is natural (and perhaps praiseworthy) for educated minds to support the small, the weak and the downtrodden, but there are often gins and snares. Conor Cruise O'Brien noted … that we ought not to "idealise minorities, or to forget that today's underdog may be tomorrow's power-crazed bully" and there are, surely, many historical and contemporary contexts which bear him out. (1996, p. 33)

The issues of language rights and language oppression apply to all individuals and groups, and must do so equally if they are to have any meaning at all (see Phillipson, Rannut, & Skutnabb-Kangas, 1995, pp. 3-4).

Our discussion thus far has emphasized language rights and violations of language rights, but this is really only one side of the coin. We can also talk about the language responsibilities of both the individual and the society, and this is an important, if often overlooked, aspect of the debates about linguistic human rights. If the individual has the *right* to an education in his or her native language, he or she also has a *responsibility* (or *obligation*) to learn the socially dominant language of his or her society. Similarly, while a society is certainly within its rights to legislate an official language, it then must recognize that it has the related *obligation* to provide the educational support necessary to ensure that all of its members have access to this language. There is, in short, a fundamental assumption in the discourse about language rights that such rights are matched by obligations on the part of both the individual and the society—as, indeed, are all human rights.

LANGUAGE RIGHTS IN U.S. PUBLIC EDUCATION

At the present time, the U.S. Constitution makes no direct reference whatsoever to language or to language rights; such rights are presumed to be inherent in other legal and constitutional protections. Indeed, it is this lack of specific mention of language rights that is, to some extent, at issue in contemporary debates about adopting English as the official language of the United States (see Baron, 1990; Crawford, 1992a, 1992b). With respect to education in the United States, I would argue that language rights (as well as concomitant language responsibilities) are both logically and practically necessary conditions for the provision of fair and equitable education for all children in our society, as well as required by our international commitments to human rights. In practice, this would entail the right of the individual to use his or her language in various contexts, including but certainly not limited to the use of the native language as the medium of instruction as appropriate. At the same time, it would also entail ensuring access to the socially, economically and politically dominant language of the society. Thus, educational programs that promote linguistic diversity while at the same time ensuring that all students gain competence in the socially dominant language would be required.

Such is not, however, the reality. Henry Trueba recently noted that, "there are approximately 35 million persons in the United States who speak a language other than English at home, of whom about 20 million are not fluent in English. Almost 11 million of them are school age children" (1991, p. 45). These numbers alone are significant, but they take on even greater urgency when one takes into account the demographic and social trends that they represent. Both the percentage and absolute number of limited English proficiency students in the public schools—both those explicitly identified by the schools as nonspeakers of English and those not so identified but nonetheless with English as a nondominant language—will increase dramatically in the years ahead as American society itself continues to become increasingly diverse (see Ager, Muskens, & Wright, 1993; Colin Baker, 2001; Corson, 1993). These children bring with them educational needs that are distinct from their English-speaking classmates, of course, and it is with their educational needs that debates about methodology (bilingual education vs. English as a Second Language, and so on) are most often concerned. If one takes into account The Declaration on the Rights of Persons Belonging to National or Ethnic, Religious and Linguistic Minorities, however, then the issue becomes less one of methodology and more one of language rights. Specifically, such children are entitled to the right to both use and learn their mother tongue in school, as well as having the right to acquire the socially dominant language. Thus, traditional "subtractive" programs in the American context, which have as their principal (and often only) objective the acquisition of English are simply incompatible with the articulated conceptions of language rights as they apply to minority language children.

Another issue that must be raised here is that of the problem of elitism and language status. In the U.S. context, it is clear that there is an unarticulated but nonetheless powerful hierarchy of languages and language varieties, with varieties of standard (or mainstream) English at the top of the hierarchy. This hierarchy is important both in terms of the attitudes of educational institutions and educators, as well as with respect to its implications for the perceptions of speakers of languages other than English (see Reagan & Osborn, 1998). For example, Castilian Spanish is generally viewed favorably, while Puerto Rican Spanish is not. This, in turn, leads to radically different views of bilingualism. For a native speaker of English to acquire competence in Spanish, for instance, is seen as not only positive, but impressive and relatively noteworthy. For a native speaker of Spanish to acquire competence in English in the U.S. setting, though, is largely taken for granted—and if such a person does *not* acquire competence in English, this is then seen as a deficiency.

One of the most interesting and challenging aspects of dealing with matters of language and language diversity in the U.S. context is that of ideological monolingualism. In essence, this refers to a set of commonly held beliefs about language among many (perhaps most) English-speakers in our society. Dell Hymes has identified what he takes to be six core, albeit generally tacit, assumptions about language in the United States:

- everyone in the United States speaks only English, or should;
- bilingualism is inherently unstable, probably injurious, and possibly unnatural;
- foreign literary languages can be respectively studied, but not foreign languages in their domestic varieties (it is one thing to study the French spoken in Paris, another to study the French spoken in Louisiana);
- most everyone else in the world is learning English anyway, and that, together with American military and economic power, makes it unnecessary to worry about knowing the language of a country in which one has business, bases, or hostages;
- differences in language are essentially of two kinds, right and wrong; and
- verbal fluency and noticeable style are suspicious, except as entertainment (1996, pp. 84-85).

Each of these assumptions is fundamentally flawed, and the list as a whole is grounded in a lack of understanding of the nature of language, a confusion of historical mythology with historical fact, and is replete with both factual and normative errors. Nevertheless, the belief system that undergirds and supports ideological monolingualism is very powerful, and has direct implications for such educational issues as the role and purpose of second/foreign language education in the schools, the place of language and language study in multicultural and global education programs, how the schools deal with the presence of nonmainstream varieties of English, how they seek to meet the needs of children whose native language is other than English, and, of course, with respect to second/foreign language education broadly conceived. What is at issue here, of course, is really the nexus of linguistics and politics, which explains the extent to which such matters become the focus of language, social, and educational conflict.

The situation with respect to language rights is arguably even more complex in the specific case of the Deaf[1] in the United States. Unlike other minority language communities, the Deaf are unique in that their language and culture are, in the vast majority of instances, transmitted not from one generation to the next, but rather from peer to peer. The community is also distinct in that its members have differential access to the society's dominant language due not so much to social, economic, educational, or political factors, but rather to factors directly attributable to their physiological condition.

There are, broadly speaking, two quite different ways to view deafness, one a medical model which focuses on the audiological element of deafness, and the other a sociocultural model which is grounded in a view of Deafness as a cultural and linguistic condition. These two perspectives on deafness lead to two very different approaches to language rights as they apply to the case of the deaf: compensatory and empowerment approaches to language rights. Compensatory approaches are those which are grounded in the medical model of deafness, while empowerment approaches are grounded in the sociocultural model of deafness. Compensatory approaches, in short, assume a deficit view of deafness, while empowerment approaches assume a difference view of deafness. Conceptualizations of language rights for the deaf, as well as language policies targeting the deaf, inevitably reflect one of these two approaches.

Our focus here is on *cultural* Deafness, in contrast to what might be termed audiological deafness. As Harlan Lane has cogently explained in his book *The Mask of Benevolence: Disabling the Deaf Community*,

> Most Americans who have impaired hearing are not members of the American deaf community. They were acculturated to hearing society, their first language was a spoken one, and they became hard of hearing or deaf in the course of their lives, often late in life. This book is not about them; it is about people who grow up deaf, acculturated to the manual language and society of the deaf community. (1992, p. xi)

Precisely the same distinction applies in the case of the argument presented here. The position taken here applies to those individuals who identify themselves as members of the Deaf cultural community, and who choose to use a natural sign language as their vernacular language. Others, and especially those who experience audiological losses well into their lives, are thus excluded from our focus here. This does not mean that the matter of language rights is irrelevant for such individuals; quite the contrary is the case. However, for such people the debate about compensatory versus empowerment approaches is simply not appropriate: for them, compensation is indeed what is at stake.

The dominant perspective on deafness in most societies around the world is grounded in the view that deafness is essentially a medical condition, characterized by an auditory deficit (that is, deaf people are people who cannot hear). This medical model of deafness leads naturally to efforts to try to remediate the deficit. In short, the medical model is premised on the idea that deaf people are not only different from hearing people, but that they are, at least in a physiological sense, *inferior* to hearing people. If one accepts the medical model of deafness, and the myriad assumptions which undergird it, then the only reasonable approach to dealing with deafness is indeed to attempt to remediate the problem, which is, of course, precisely what is done when one focuses on the teaching of speech and lip reading in education, utilizes hearing aids to maximize whatever residual hearing a deaf individual may possess, and seeks to develop medical solutions (such as cochlear implants) to hearing impairment. In other words, the medical model of deafness would seem inevitably to lead to efforts to try to help the deaf individual to become as like a hearing person as possible. This medical model of deafness has been labeled a *pathological* model by a number of writers, and it clearly is so at least insofar as deaf individuals who see themselves in cultural and linguistic terms, and for whom signed language is the language of choice, are concerned.

The medical model of deafness is by far the more common approach to understanding deafness and deaf people, and is, in fact, for many hearing people little more than common sense. In contrast, though, the idea that the Deaf are a cultural and linguistic minority group (and, indeed, an *oppressed* cultural and linguistic minority group at that), is one that challenges many assumptions and preconceptions about both the nature of language and culture and of disability. And yet, the view of Deaf people as a cultural community comparable in many ways to other cultural communities is one that has gained considerable support and credibility in both the United States (see Erting, 1985; Reagan, 1990, 1995b, 1996; Sacks, 1989; Schein, 1989; Wilcox, 1989), and it is to a brief discussion of this perspective on deafness that I now turn.

One of the more intriguing aspects of any discussion of the Deaf as a cultural and linguistic community, of course, is the *need* to make a case that there really is such a thing as *Deaf culture*, just as one sometimes needs to build a case for American Sign Language being a *real* language.[2] The need for such discussions tells us a great deal already; not, perhaps, so much about the Deaf as about the stereotypes and biases of the hearing world, and about issues of power, paternalism, and cultural imperialism (see Hahn, 1986; Wilcox, 1987). In order to avoid such paternalism, writers on Deaf culture have attempted to deal with the world of the deaf from what is basically an anthropological perspective, focusing on the ways in which Deaf people themselves see their world (see Padden & Humphries, 1988). In short, what Padden and Humphries and others have compellingly argued is that the Deaf cultural community is characterized by the same kinds of elements that characterize any other cultural community, amongst which are a common, shared language, a shared awareness of cultural identity, distinctive behavioral norms and patterns, cultural artifacts, endogamous marital patterns, a shared historical knowledge and awareness, and a network of voluntary, in-group social organizations (see Reagan, 1995b, 1996).

The single most significant component of Deaf cultural identity in most societies is competence in a natural sign language, the community's vernacular language as well as a powerful marker of in-group membership and group solidarity (see Charolette Baker & Cokely, 1980: Erting, 1978; Kannapell, 1993; Padden, 1980; Lucas & Valli, 1992). It is important to note here, though, that this applies only to *natural* sign languages; other commonly used types of signing, including both the pidgin sign language normally employed by hearing signers and the artificially constructed manual sign codes for spoken languages often used in educational settings, fulfill very different functions and are viewed very differently by the Deaf community (see Lucas, 1989; Lucas & Valli, 1992; Reagan, 1995a; Stewart & Akamatsu, 1988). Without going into unnecessary detail here, pidgin sign is generally seen by the Deaf as an appropriate means of communication with hearing individuals, while manual sign codes are widely rejected by the Deaf as awkward efforts to impose the structures of a spoken language on sign (see Ramsey, 1989).

Deaf communities are in fact diglossic in that there is widespread bilingualism, involving both spoken and signed language, and in that these two kinds of languages are generally used in somewhat different settings and for somewhat different purposes (see Lucas & Valli, 1992, pp. 21-23). The bilingualism that characterizes such communities is in fact a *social* bilingualism rather than necessarily an *individual* bilingualism, since not all members of the community are in fact functionally bilingual (see John Edwards, 1994, pp. 83-86). As an educational objective, however, it is certainly the case that functional individual bilingualism makes a good deal of sense. As Danielle Bouvet has argued,

> While true bilingualism is linguistically harmless for ordinary children, it is linguistically necessary for deaf children. Only through bilingualism can deaf children acquire speech naturally, for it exposes them to a visual language in which they do not experience any limitations in the language acquisition process.... As far as deaf children are concerned, bilingualism is the only road to healthy speech development. (1990, p. 135)

This discussion brings us to the matter of language rights and the Deaf. The medical and sociocultural perspectives of deafness not only lead to different understandings of deafness and the deaf, and to different social and educational policies for the deaf (see Baynton, 1996; Johnson, Liddell, & Erting, 1989; Safford & Safford, 1996, pp. 90-121; Walworth, Moores, & O'Rourke, 1992), but also lead to very different approaches to the issue of language rights in the Deaf community. For those accepting a medical model of deafness, discussion of language rights are, basically, irrelevant. The deaf do not constitute a minority group in the sense intended in the passages, but rather, are seen as disadvantaged members of a particular spoken language community. Thus, the medical perspective leads to what is essentially a compensatory view of language rights, which will focus on ensuring access through what is assumed to be a common language. This means that interpreting services and similar support will be provided to the deaf, because this is a way of compensating for a deficit. Although certainly well-meaning, such an approach is of course profoundly paternalistic, and are clearly grounded in a understanding of deafness as a disability.

The alternative conceptualization of language rights and the Deaf, which has been forcefully articulated by Tove Skutnabb-Kangas (1994) among others, is grounded in the sociocultural view of deafness. The sociocultural view of deafness leads to an empowerment approach to language rights for the deaf, in which signed language and other supports are called for not as a means to correct a disability, but rather because the Deaf, as a cultural and linguistic minority, should be entitled to them as basic human rights (see Nover, 1995). Also at issue here, of course, is the matter of how one defines *mother tongue* in the context of the deaf child; a matter of no little complexity, to be sure (see Bouvet, 1990, pp. 119-133, for a very thorough discussion of this topic). Here, then, the United Nation's Declaration of the Rights of Persons Belonging to National or Ethnic, Religious and Linguistic Minorities is clearly relevant, even though, as Harlan Lane and his colleagues have argued, internationally recognized language rights are "almost universally violated when it comes to signed language minorities" (Lane, Hoffmeister, & Bahan, 1996, p. 422). Recent efforts in various states in the United States to have American Sign Language declared a *real* language,[3] are illustrative of manifestations of this empowerment perspective on language rights for the Deaf. Implicit in this empowerment perspective on language rights for the deaf, of course, is a rejection of the compensatory perspective as either a sort of linguistic imperialism, or perhaps even cultural and linguistic genocide (see Skutnabb-Kangas, 1994).

Thus far, I have suggested that compensatory and empowerment approaches to language rights for the deaf are representative of basically incompatible views of both deafness and language rights. Although a case might be made for these two perspectives constituting what philosophers of science sometimes call incomensurable paradigms, political practice in the real world is somewhat more complex and confused. This is the case, in part, because resources in our society tend to be more readily available for disabled groups than they are for cultural and linguistic minorities (and especially for very small cultural and linguistic minorities). Thus, in the case of the deaf it is often politically and financially expedient to accept the status and labels of disability, even while advocating for recognition of the deaf as a nondisabled (or, to use politically correct terminology, a *differently-abled*) cultural and linguistic community. In short, there is a generally unarticulated tension with respect to the rights of the deaf: the cost of political recognition as a cultural and linguistic minority group may well be far greater, for the average deaf person, than the benefits of tolerating the paternalism (and even pity) of the hearing majority (see Shapiro, 1993; Wrigley, 1997). Compensatory approaches to language rights, then, may actually in some circumstances be somewhat empowering, even as empowerment approaches may prove to be disempowering.

IMPLICATIONS FOR SCHOOL PRACTICE

And so where, one might well ask, does all of this leave us? What implications for educational practice might one be able to draw from our discussion of language rights? Certainly the importance and, indeed, the centrality of issues of language and language rights in the educational sphere is a powerful and important lesson, and one that is often overlooked in discussions of educational practice. Language rights in the educational sphere are an important element in the development of educational language policies, as David Corson made clear in a number of works (see Corson, 1999, 2001). Beyond this, though, our discussion points to a key area of need with respect to teacher education: the need for greater awareness and sensitivity to language issues, matters of language dominance and oppression, matters of language attitudes and bias, and both implicit and explicit assumptions about language that are widely shared by educators and the public (see also Reagan, 1997a). In other words, what is required is a greater concern with and focus on what some scholars have called *critical language awareness*: an understanding of the relationship between language and power in society, as well as a wariness to accept unquestioningly technicist approaches and solutions to language *problems* that mask or hide underlying political, economic, and ideological agendas (see Andrews, 1998; Fairclough, 1989, 1995; Gunnarsson, Linell, & Nordberg, 1997; Janks, 1991, 1997; van Lier, 1995;

Wilkinson & Janks, 1998). The real issue with respect to language rights is to help students recognize that, as James Russell Lowell noted in 1844, "They have rights who dare maintain them." It is our job to help our students maintain and exercise their rights, regardless of the social or political pressures to do otherwise.

NOTES

1. A common distinction made in writing about deafness is between *deaf* and *Deaf*: the former refers to deafness solely as an audiological condition, the latter to deafness as a cultural condition. The basic idea underlying this distinction is that when writing about cultural groups in general, upper case letters are employed (African American, Hispanic, etc.). Thus, a person can be *deaf* without being *Deaf* (as in the case of an older person who gradually loses his/her hearing).
2. In recent years, for example, there have been ongoing debates in many parts of the United States about whether American Sign Language (ASL) should be offered as a second/foreign language in secondary schools and in colleges and universities. Central to these debates has been the question of whether ASL is in some sense less *real* or *legitimate* than spoken languages—a position that ignores more than 30 years of linguistic research on the nature, structure, and uses of ASL (see Reagan, 1992b, 1997b; Wilcox, 1988; Wilcox & Wilcox, 1997).
3. The recognition of ASL as a real language, generally for purposes of academic foreign language credit (especially with respect to secondary schools), is one that has been gradually taking place in the United States on a state-by-state basis (see Wilcox, 1988). Jacobs (1996, pp. 217-226) provides a detailed analysis of the status of ASL in each of the 50 states. Although well intended and clearly supported by the Deaf themselves, such efforts have the potential to do positive harm as well as good. As Jeffrey Nash has argued, "since ASL has been maintained in spite of and perhaps to a degree because of oppressive language policies, such official recognition of ASL may not be necessary, and could even have unintended consequences of changing the social functions of ASL. ASL functions as the cement of the community because of the symbolic identity it offers to deaf people—an identity which contrasts markedly with those they receive from having been members of educational institutions.... As long as deaf people feel a need to create for themselves distinctive identities, they will rely on ASL as their medium for social contact. Conversely, if ASL were to become an official language of instruction in special education programs in the United States, it might lose some of its power as a device for accomplishing a distinctive social identity" (1987, p. 20).

CHAPTER 5

WHY CAN'T I TAKE RUSSIAN AT SCHOOL?

Commonly and Less Commonly Taught Languages

Language is not only an instrument for the communication of messages. This becomes especially clear in multilingual communities where various groups have their own language: e.g. the Flemish in Belgium and the Gujeratis in India. With its language a group distinguishes itself. The cultural norms and values of a group are transmitted by its language. Group feelings are emphasized by using the group's own language, and members of the outgroup are excluded from its internal transactions.

—*René Appel and Pieter Muysken* (1987, p. 11)

Several years ago, after hearing me converse with a friend in Russian, my son asked me what language we had been speaking. I told him, and he asked whether he could study Russian at his school, since he and his classmates were to began studying a second/foreign language in fifth grade, the next school year. I explained that the only languages that he could choose from were French and Spanish, and in an irritated voice he asked, "Why can't I study *Russian* at school?" His question was in fact a very good one, and one for which I did not have an answer that either of us found

Critical Questions, Critical Perspectives:
Language and the Second Language Educator, 59–76

particularly compelling. The fundamental issue at stake was not, of course, why Russian in particular was not offered (it is, after all, offered in some districts, albeit far less frequently than French or Spanish), but rather, was one of how we as a society have determined which languages are to be taught in the public schools. This is an intriguing question, especially when one takes into account a demographic perspective on languages in education, as suggested by Walker:

> Ninety-seven percent of the students of modern foreign languages in the public schools of this country are studying Spanish, French, and German.... In American colleges and universities, Spanish, French and German enroll approximately eighty-five percent of the students of foreign languages.... A rough calculation presents a startling aspect of educational practice in the United States: *At least ninety-one percent of the academic study of foreign languages is directed toward languages used by twelve to thirteen percent of humanity.* (1989, p. 111, emphasis mine)

Estimates of the number of languages spoken around the world vary dramatically, generally ranging somewhere between 3,000 and 8,000, with the most reasonable estimates in the neighborhood of 4,500 to 6,000 separate and distinct languages. This range of estimates is obviously considerable; John Edwards has attempted to explain it in the following manner:

> What accounts for this large variability? There are four main factors of importance: inadequate basic knowledge, the "dead or alive" distinction, the "naming" problem and, perhaps most salient, the language-dialect dimension (the last three are all specific instances of the first general point). (1994, p. 19)

What is especially interesting about these numbers, from the perspective of a second/foreign language educator, is how incredibly few of this substantial number of different languages are commonly (or even less than commonly) taught in the context of second/foreign language education programs.[1] To be sure, although linguists stress the fundamental equality of languages, some languages are clearly, in social, demographic, economic, and political terms, "more equal" than others (Altmann, 1997, pp. 226-233; see also Pennycook, 1994; Phillipson, 1992; Wardhaugh, 1987). Using simply the number of native speakers as the selection criterion, the 10 largest languages in the world are, in order, Mandarin, English, Hindi, Spanish, Russian, Arabic, Bengali, Portuguese, Japanese, and French (Fromkin & Rodman, 1993, pp. 351-354). If one takes into account languages that are widely used as second languages, then the list changes somewhat, and our focus becomes the *languages of wider communication* (generally taken to include English, French, Spanish, Russian, Arabic, and German).

In the context of public schooling in the United States, only three of these languages—French, German, and Spanish—are, together with Latin, commonly offered as second/foreign languages. Draper and Hicks (1996) have documented that fewer than half of all secondary students in American public schools study a second/foreign language. Of the six million students in middle and secondary schools who *do* study a second/foreign language, roughly 65% study Spanish, 22% study French, 6% study German, and 3.5% study Latin. The remaining 3.5% of students study a wide variety of languages, the *less commonly taught languages*. It is with the languages studied by this 3.5% of the student population, as well as those not studied at all, that this chapter will be concerned. Specifically, I want to attempt to outline what might be called a *social grammar* of the less commonly taught languages.[2] In other words, the social, political, economic, cultural, and ideological elements affecting these languages, especially in terms of their presence or lack of presence in the public school curriculum, will be explored, and a model will be offered for understanding the implicit, albeit generally unarticulated, linguistic hierarchy that seems to exist with respect to the less commonly taught languages.

There are a number of compelling reasons for second/foreign language educators to be interested in and concerned with the teaching and learning of the less commonly taught languages. First and foremost, at least in terms of making a public case for the less commonly taught languages, is what can be called the geopolitical aspect of language teaching and learning. In essence, it is in the best interest of the society to produce sufficient numbers of linguistically competent individuals to function in the various national and regional languages that are used in areas of national political, economic, and strategic concern. It was with just such concerns in mind that the U.S. government in 1985 identified a list of some 169 "critical languages," languages which "would promote important scientific research or security interests of a national or economic kind" (Crystal, 1987, p. 342). The teaching and learning of Russian and, to a somewhat lesser extent, Chinese, has been supported by geopolitical concerns in the past, and the recent efforts to increase the number of speakers of Arabic in the United States are similarly motivated.

Furthermore, the less commonly taught languages are important in terms of their speaker communities, and in terms of our ability to understand these communities. As Robert Bunge has clearly and compellingly argued, "language is not just another thing we do as humans; it is *the* thing we do. It is a total environment; we live in the language as a fish lives in water. It is the audible and visible manifestation of the soul of a people" (1992, p. 376, emphasis in original). It would, in short, be difficult to overstate the centrality of language to worldview and both group and individual identity.

There are also practical pedagogical lessons to be learned from the less commonly taught languages. As Roger Allen has explained with respect to teachers of Arabic, the contributions that teachers of non-Western languages:

> may have for language teaching have until recently been ignored by the profession at large. It does not seem an exaggeration to claim that one of the results of the proficiency movement has been to bring the issues raised by the non-Western, less commonly taught, "critical", "exotic" languages very much to the attention of the language-teaching profession as a whole. (1992, pp. 236-237)

Although one might argue that Allen is perhaps overly optimistic in terms of the extent to which the less commonly taught languages have been taken seriously by most language educators in the United States, his fundamental point is nevertheless well taken. There can be little doubt that teachers of less commonly taught languages bring with them very different sets of experiences with respect to second/foreign language pedagogy, and the discussion about and reflection on their experiences is almost certain to benefit both less commonly taught language teachers and teachers of the more commonly taught languages (see Ihde, 1997).

Beyond these lessons for language education, though, the teaching and learning of less commonly taught languages also impacts on education in a number of other areas, among which are multicultural education programs, global education programs, critical language, and language awareness programs (including FLEX programs at the elementary level), and, as will be discussed later in this chapter, what might be called *political education*.

UNDERSTANDING *GRAMMAR* METAPHORICALLY

Metaphors can provide powerful and useful tools in clarifying complex ideas and arguments. As George Lakoff and Mark Johnson argued in their landmark work *Metaphors We Live By*,

> metaphor pervades our normal conceptual system. Because so many of the concepts that are important to us are either abstract or not clearly delineated in our experience ... we need to get a grasp on them by means of other concepts that we understand in clearer terms. (1980, p. 115)

The main purpose of this chapter is to provide a critical analysis of the various extralinguistic elements that affect the teaching and learning of the less commonly taught languages in the United States, especially with respect to which languages are offered and which are not offered in particular settings. The concept of a *grammar*, used in a metaphorical sense, has a great deal of explanatory power in this context. Grammars, in a literal linguistic sense, "aim to be *descriptive* and even *explanatory*, i.e., embedded within a general theory that offers principled reasons why natural languages are the way they are" (Audi, 1995, p. 302, emphasis in original), and further, are fundamentally tacit (that is, unarticulated) in nature (O'Grady & Dobrovolsky, 1996, pp. 9-10). The term *grammar*, though, can be employed not only in this strict linguistic sense, but also metaphorically, to refer to a set of generally unconscious, unarticulated rules which guide practice (see Spivey, 1997). It is in this metaphorical sense that the term is sometimes used in other scholarly disciplines to describe systematic descriptions and explanations of the tacit rules and social conventions that provide the conceptual and operational framework for a discipline or paradigm.

It is, then, in this metaphorical sense that the philosopher Wittgenstein could talk about "philosophical grammar," both in his book by that title (1974) and in the *Tractatus logico-philosophicus* (1961). Similarly, it is in a fundamentally metaphorical sense that Tzvetan Todorov (1969) utilized the concept of grammar in his masterful work *Grammaire du Décaméron* (see also Hawkes, 1977). His argument, in a nutshell, was that, "not only all languages, but also all signifying systems conform to the same grammar. It is universal not only because it informs all the languages of the universe, but because it also coincides with the structure of the universe itself" (Todorov, 1969, p. 15, my translation). It was also in this metaphorical sense that Dell Hymes could write about the "narrative form as a grammar of experience" (Hymes, 1996, pp. 121-141). Finally, the metaphorical usage of the concept of grammar has been widely employed in the literature of the philosophy of science. For example, in his description of Galileo's efforts to alter radically the traditional, Ptolemaic grammar of astronomy, Paul Feyerabend writes that:

> His motive was the wish to accommodate the Copernican point of view. Copernicanism clashes with some obvious facts, it is inconsistent with plausible, and apparently well-established, principles, and it does not fit in with the "grammar" of a commonly spoken idiom. It does not fit in with the "form of life" that contains these facts, principles, and grammatical rules. But neither the rules, nor the principles, nor even the facts are sancrosanct. We may therefore change them, create new facts and new grammatical rules, and see what happens once these rules are available and have become familiar. (1978, p. 163)

In the context of the present argument, I wish to utilize the concept of a *social grammar* to refer to the wide array of nonlinguistic and extralinguistic factors that seem to be related to the ways in which less commonly taught languages, as a group, are distinguished from the more commonly taught languages, as well as how different less commonly taught languages are viewed comparatively. In order to accomplish this end, however, we need first to explore the way in which the less commonly taught languages have been traditionally conceptualized, and it is to that discussion that we now turn.

THE TRADITIONAL CONCEPTUALIZATION OF THE LESS COMMONLY TAUGHT LANGUAGES

In a widely-cited article, Walker (1989) has argued that, at least in the U.S. context, there is a fundamental distinction made between the "traditionally taught languages" (i.e., French, Spanish and German) and all other languages (the less commonly taught languages). Although it is not uncommon for the less commonly taught languages to be grouped together in this manner as something of a miscellaneous, catch-all category (see, e.g., Crookes, Sakka, Shiroma, & Ye, 1991; Everson, 1993; Ryding, 1989; Walker, 1991), this is inevitably misleading on a number of grounds, not the least of which is the problem of grouping together radically different *kinds* of languages. Indeed, Walker has suggested that "thinking of less commonly taught languages as a category of language is like thinking of 'nonelephants' as a category of animals" (1989, p. 111). Walton, in attempting to address this problem, has suggested that the less commonly taught languages can be best understood as being divided in practice into three subgroups (1) less commonly taught European languages such as Russian, Italian, Portuguese, and Swedish; (2) higher-enrollment non-Indo-European languages, such as Arabic, Chinese, and Japanese; and (3) lower-enrollment non-Indo-European languages such as Burmese, Indonesian, and Swahili (1992, p. 1).

Jordan and Walton (1987) have even gone so far as to label groups 2 and 3 as the "truly foreign languages," emphasizing their presumed difficulty and degree of difference from English, and Jacobs (1996), in what could be considered a sort of linguistic one-upmanship, has offered an argument for the inclusion of American Sign Language in one of these categories as well. The key criterion that seems to be applied in making these distinctions is essentially the distance from English, in terms of such factors as phonology, grammar, lexicon, orthography, and spelling (see Hawkins, 1981, pp. 79-82; James, 1979). Utilizing a five-point rating scale, the interlingual distance between any two languages can be deter-

Table 5.1. Interlingual Distance to English of Selected Languages

	Interlingual Distance to English				
Factor	*1*	*2*	*3*	*4*	*5*
Phonology	Italian	German/ Spanish	Russian	French	—
Grammar	—	French/ Italian/ Spanish	German/ Russian	—	—
Lexicon	French/ Italian/ Spanish	German	—	Russian	—
Orthography	French/ German/ Italian/ Spanish	—	—	Russian	—
Spelling	Italian/ Spanish	German/ Russian	—	French	—

mined and assigned a quantitative rating. Thus, in an analysis of the interlingual distances of English to French, German, Italian, Russian and Spanish, James (1979) determined the following global scores (see Table 5.1):

French	12
German	10
Italian	6
Russian	16
Spanish	7

Thus, Italian and Spanish would be relatively easier languages for an English speaker to learn than would be French or German, with Russian constituting the most difficult in James' sample. These results are actually fairly consistent with the Educational Testing Service's (ETS) estimates of the classroom time required to meet various levels of linguistic proficiency in different languages (see Liskin-Gasparro, 1982; Omaggio Hadley, 2001). Basically, the ETS estimates divide target languages into four groups, ranging from those which are most quickly acquired by English speakers to those that require the most time (see Table 5.2).[3]

While the division of less commonly taught languages by degree of difficulty for English speakers does make a certain amount of sense, it does not move us forward in terms of understanding why certain less com-

Table 5.2. Language Learning Difficulty, By Group

Group I:	Afrikaans, Danish, Dutch, French, Haitian Creole, Italian, Norwegian, Portuguese, Romanian, Spanish, Swahili, Swedish
Group II:	Bulgarian, Dari, Farsi, German, Greek, Hindi, Indonesian, Malay, Urdu
Group III:	Amharic, Bengali, Burmese, Czech, Finnish, Hebrew, Hungarian, Khmer, Lao, Nepali, Pilipino, Polish, Russian, Serbo-Croation, Sinhala, Thai, Tamil, Turkish, Vietnamese
Group IV:	Arabic, Chinese, Japanese, Korean

monly taught languages are more popular than others. If interlingual distance was really all that was at stake, then we would expect languages in ETS Group I to be considerably more common than those in Group IV—and yet, that does not appear to be the case. Three of the four listed languages in Group IV (Arabic, Chinese, and Japanese) are among the more popular less commonly taught languages, while Group I includes a large number of languages that are virtually never taught as second/foreign languages in U.S. public schools (e.g., Afrikaans, Danish, Dutch, Norwegian, Romanian, Swedish), despite their presumed relative ease of acquisition. The problem, of course, is that decisions and choices about language are rarely made simply on grounds of ease of learning or what might be called "hierarchies of difficulty" (see DiPietro, 1971, pp. 161-164); rather, such choices are deeply grounded and embedded in social, cultural, economic, political, demographic, and ideological beliefs and attitudes. It is in order to achieve a better understanding of these extralinguistic factors that guide language choice that a social grammar of the less commonly taught languages is needed.

OUTLINE OF A SOCIAL GRAMMAR OF THE LESS COMMONLY TAUGHT LANGUAGES

If ease of acquisition (as indicated by interlingual distance) does not provide a satisfactory explanation for why some less commonly taught languages are found in public school curricula in the United States, and others are not, then what could explain this difference? The answer requires a social grammar of the less commonly taught languages; that is to say, what is needed is a framework within which such factors as social, cultural, economic, political, demographic, and ideological beliefs and attitudes can be taken into account. Implicit in such a framework, of course, is the huge gap between the perceptions, attitudes, and beliefs of linguists and the general public with regard to language. This gap can be seen quite clearly, for instance, in Einar Haugen's introduction to his book *Blessings of Babel.* After recounting the biblical story of the Tower of Babel, Haugen notes that:

> Those of us who love languages, especially if we have devoted our lives to learning or teaching them, find it hard to put ourselves in the right frame of mind to understand the concept of language diversity as a curse. We see in language a source of novel delights and subtle experience, a blessing. (Haugen, 1987, p. 1)

Speaking both personally and professionally, I find myself in strong agreement with Haugen—and yet I recognize that this view is far from the dominant one in contemporary American society, as we saw demonstrated in the previous chapter with Dell Hymes' identification of the common assumptions about language in the United States. They were:

- Everyone in the United States speaks only English, or should.
- Bilingualism is inherently unstable, probably injurious, and possibly unnatural.
- Foreign literary languages can be respectively studied, but not foreign languages in their domestic varieties (it is one thing to study the French spoken in Paris, another to study the French spoken in Louisiana).
- Most everyone else in the world is learning English anyway, and that, together with American military and economic power, makes it unnecessary to worry about knowing the language of a country in which one has business, bases, or hostages.
- Differences in language are essentially of two kinds, right and wrong.
- Verbal fluency and noticeable style are suspicious, except as entertainment (it's what you mean that counts). (Hymes, 1996, pp. 84-85)

The problems with each of these assumptions notwithstanding, Hymes' list nevertheless *does,* in my view, fairly accurately reflect commonly held beliefs about language in the United States.

Although Hymes' analysis may help to contextualize a social grammar of the less commonly taught languages, on its own it is obviously far from sufficient for this purpose, as indeed are the related, and conceptually powerful, notions of linguistic imperialism and linguicism (see, e.g., Phillipson, 1988, 1992, pp. 50-57; Skutnabb-Kangas, 1988; Tollefson, 1995). Rather, what is needed is a framework for classifying the less commonly taught languages, coupled with a discussion of the explanatory factors for why particular less commonly taught languages fall where they do within this framework. It is to a discussion of such a framework that we now turn.

It is clear that there is a hierarchy of less commonly taught languages, but it is also clear, as was discussed above, that this hierarchy is not one grounded in linguistic factors. In order to be useful, the hierarchy of less commonly taught languages is better envisaged as one reflecting the likelihood of a particular less commonly taught language being offered as a second/foreign language option in a public school. Thus, looking at second/foreign language education in the United States as a whole, we can talk about a hierarchy of five levels:

Level 1 *Commonly Taught Languages*
Level 2 *Most Commonly Taught "Less Commonly Taught Languages"*
Level 3 *Rarely Taught "Less Commonly Taught Languages"*
Level 4 *Never/Virtually Never Taught "Less Commonly Taught Languages"*
Level 5 *The "Nonlanguages"*

Level 1 refers not to less commonly taught languages at all, of course, but rather to the languages most commonly associated with second/foreign language education in the United States: French, German, Spanish, and probably Latin. Although there are significant differences with respect to student enrollment among these languages, all four are widely offered throughout the United States, certified teachers are generally readily available in all four languages (though, to be sure, there are periodic and regional shortages), a variety of textbooks and supplementary pedagogical materials are available for all four languages, curricular guides are widely available and thorough, and all four languages are seen as fully legitimate objects of study. To a very significant extent, when one talks about second/foreign language education in the United States, it is with these languages that one is most explicitly concerned.

Level 2 encompasses the less commonly taught languages that fairly routinely appear in public school curricula in most if not all parts of the United States, albeit considerably less frequently than even Latin and serving far fewer students. Included among the Level 2 languages would be Russian, Chinese, Japanese, and Arabic. It is interesting to note that these languages, the most commonly taught of the less commonly taught languages, all involve substantial orthographic challenges for English-speaking students, and all involve considerable interlingual distance from English (though Russian is obviously, on both counts, demonstrably easier for English speakers than the other languages). Although shortages certainly exist, teacher certification in Level 2 languages is commonly possible and such teachers do exist, textbooks and supportive materials are available, and curricular guides have been prepared in many states and local school districts.

Level 3 refers to the less commonly taught languages that do, on occasion, make their way into the public school curricula, but do so fairly rarely (even when compared with the Level 2 less commonly taught languages), and often in geographically restricted contexts. Included here would be such heritage languages as Polish, Italian, Portuguese, Modern Greek, Hawai'ian, Norwegian, and so on. The key here is that, for the most part, these languages are offered where they are reflective of some element of the ethnic composition and makeup of the local population. In other words, to some extent Level 3 less commonly taught languages are actually examples of ethnic language maintenance or revival efforts as much as second/foreign language efforts. Teaching certification is uncommon for Level 3 languages, and very often nonlanguage educators who speak the target language are utilized to teach these languages. Textbooks and supplementary teaching materials are available, but limited, and few formal curricular guidelines exist for most Level 3 languages.

Level 4 is by far the largest and most inclusive category, and would include the overwhelming majority of the world's languages. Examples of Level 4 languages would include virtually all African languages,[4] most Asian and Oceanic languages, indigenous Amerind languages, and many smaller European languages, among others—the overwhelming percentage of which, incidentally, would constitute endangered languages (see Hale, 1998). This is, to some extent, a category of exclusion, in that it includes all languages that do not fit anywhere else. What holds this very large and diverse group of languages together (rather as a category of "nonelephants,", as Walker, 1989, would have it) is that they are virtually never (or never) offered as second/foreign language options in American public schools. As a general rule, teaching certification is not even possible in these languages, textbooks and pedagogical materials are difficult to come by and often of poor quality where they exist at all, curricula for public school classes do not exist, and, perhaps most important, there tends to be virtually no interest among either students or in the community at large for offering these languages. To a considerable extent, Level 4 languages are perceived, in the American context, as simply irrelevant.

The last category, Level 5, differs from the others in that it includes what can be termed *nonlegitimate* languages—that is, languages and language varieties that society appears to view as fundamentally different from *legitimate* languages. Such a distinction is, of course, linguistically nonsensical. The idea that there can be legitimate and nonlegitimate languages makes no sense at all on any reasonable set of linguistic criteria. The distinction, though, is not a linguistic one—it is one that is all too commonly made in American society to dismiss certain languages are legitimate objects of study. Two of the better examples of this phenomenon are the cases of American Sign Language and Esperanto (see Reagan, 1997b). An especially interesting element of these Level 5 languages is the degree of controversy that often surrounds them. Both American Sign Language and Esperanto are, in fact, offered in American public schools, and yet the resistance to them is surprisingly strong and often highly emotive in nature (see Reagan, 1998; Vandenberg, 1998).

With respect to providing an explanatory model for why specific languages are located in a particular level, there are six fundamental factors which, taken together, appear to determine a language's status. Specifically, these six factors are: (1) the size of the language's speaker community; (2) the geographic spread of the language (including its use as a second language or lingua franca); (3) whether the language constitutes a heritage language in the local U.S. setting; (4) whether the language is a language of wider communication; (5) whether the language has an established and recognized literary/written tradition; and (6) whether the language is a living or dead language.[5] It is important to note here that it is the *interaction* of these six factors that determines a particular language's status; no single factor can ensure either the presence or absence of a language in the public school curriculum. Indeed, using a model such as that proposed by James (1979) for interlingual distance works quite well in applying these six factors to particular languages.

We can test the proposed model with several less commonly taught languages. Consider the following cases: Estonian, Italian, Old English, Serbian, and Zulu. What I take to be a rough approximation of the results of this application is presented in Table 5.3 (though I readily admit that the ratings in this case are largely subjective, I think that this example nonetheless demonstrates the principle with which we are concerned). Translating the results to global scores, we end up with the following:

Estonian	15
Italian	25*
Old English	9
Serbian	19
Zulu	16

What these results suggest is entirely consistent with what we already know about the relative status of these languages in the United States in general and in U.S. public education in particular: of these less commonly taught languages, only Italian would be likely to have a high enough score to appear as a second/foreign language option anywhere in American curricula. This does not mean that students might not benefit from the study of the other languages examined; indeed, a strong case could be offered for

Table 5.3. Test of Model:
Estonian, Italian, Old English, Serbian, and Zulu

	Factors Affecting the Status of Less Commonly Taught Languages in the U.S.				
	1 (Weakest)	*2*	*3*	*4*	*5 (Strongest)*
Demography of language	Old English (no living speakers)	Estonian (1 million speakers)	Zulu (7 million speakers) Serbian (15 million speakers)	Italian (66 million speakers)	
Geographic spread of language	Old English (no longer spoken; when used, restricted to parts of Britain)	Estonian (Estonia and continguous areas) Serbian (Former Yugoslavia)	Zulu (Southern Africa) Italian (Italy, contiguous areas)		
Heritage language in U.S.	Zulu	Estonian	[Old English]	Serbian Italian	
Language of wider communication	Old English	Estonian Serbian Zulu		Italian	
Established and recognized literary tradition		Old English Zulu	Serbian Estonian		Italian
Living language	Old English			Estonian	Italian Serbian Zulu

the value of English-speaking students studying Old English, or in fact, any of these languages. And yet, our own experience assures us that this is *most* unlikely—and the model proposed here helps to explain why this is so. It should be kept in mind that the relative weight of the six factors used in this model may change somewhat from time to time and place to place. Thus, the relative status of Classical Greek can be seen to have changed fairly dramatically over the past 50 years, as indeed has the status of all of the Level 2 languages. The most significant point to be made here is that none of these six factors is really linguistic in nature at all, but rather, all reflect social, cultural, political, and ideological beliefs and assumptions.

EDUCATIONAL IMPLICATIONS

The articulation of a social grammar of the less commonly taught languages has significant and timely educational implications in the U.S. context, in terms of language pedagogy, multicultural and global education efforts, and the politics of education (especially with respect to critical and emancipatory education). In terms of second/foreign language pedagogy in the United States, an examination of the extralinguistic factors which determine the relative status of particular languages is an important aspect of language studies with which second/foreign language educators, and indeed all educators, need to be familiar (see Reagan, 1997a). Language is a profoundly social activity, inevitably embedded in a cultural, political, economic, and even ideological context, and yet all too often language educators assume a narrow technicist, and essentially positivistic, view of both language and language teaching. The consideration of the status of the less commonly taught languages can help to ameliorate this situation, just as serious discussion about language teaching methods and strategies can generate important ideas and contribute to a sort of cross-fertilization among second/foreign language teachers. In the past, this cross fertilization has tended to move from the traditionally taught languages to the less commonly taught languages; a clear example of movement in this direction is Catherine Ball's interesting effort to incorporate text-based reading strategies in her teaching of Old English (see C. Ball, 1995).[6] Similarly, the development of more student-friendly textbooks in some less commonly taught languages is another obvious example of such benefits (see, for instance, the case of recent Xhosa textbooks in South Africa, such as Munnik, 1994; Pinnock, 1994; and Zotwana, 1991). The possibilities for cross-fertilization, however, are very much two-way. Indeed, as R. Allen has argued,

> As guidelines for such languages as Hebrew, Thai, Hausa, and Hindi take their place alongside Russian, Chinese, Japanese, and Arabic, we all begin to realise that teachers of languages from the various regions of the world have an enormous amount to contribute to, and learn from, each other about every aspect of their joint enterprise. (1992, p. 237)

A related area in which there is considerable potential for worthwhile interaction is between foreign language educators, teachers of English as a Second Language, and teachers working in bilingual education programs—where, incidentally, some less commonly taught languages are far more likely to appear than in the traditional second/foreign language curriculum.[7]

Multicultural and global education programs, which have become increasingly popular in the United States in recent years, are another area where concern with less commonly taught languages is relevant. The fundamental challenge in such programs, from a linguistic perspective, is the minimal concern with language and language diversity that is generally found in multicultural and global curricula. There is, to be sure, a significant difference between the two types of programs in this regard: multicultural education programs do include some concern about language minority students (see Gollnick & Chinn, 1994, pp. 219-250; Ovando, 1993), though not, for the most part, about other language issues, while global education programs tend at best to give passing mention to language issues. Indeed, in the U.S. context, global education is most commonly completely separate from second/foreign language education, and tends to be entirely monolingual in nature. As Reagan and Díaz have suggested,

> it simply does not make sense to think or talk about global education as a monolingual activity. Further ... the idea that a global education curriculum could be developed, or that a global education unit could be taught, in a monolingual fashion (as, indeed, the literature seems not merely to accept but to assume) ought to be viewed by reasonable people in roughly the same way that claims about the world being flat are viewed—in short, as utter nonsense. To propose that we can prepare students to deal with issues of internationalization and globalization exclusively through the medium of English, with little or no exposure to other languages, is rather like imagining that we can prepare students to be scientifically literate by ensuring that they read their horoscopes each day and are taught to be sure to keep their healing crystals on hand in case of illness. In short, the very message of global education would seem to require that one challenge the dominance of monolingualism in our society. (1996, pp. 7-8)

There is, however, a potential bright spot in contemporary American education, and that is the growing popularity of second/foreign language programs in elementary school contexts (see Curtain & Pesola, 1994; Lipton, 1992). Although FLES (Foreign Language in the Elementary School) programs almost always provide students with an introduction to one of the commonly taught languages (most often French or Spanish), the same is not true for FLEX (Foreign Language Exploration/Experience) programs, where the focus is more on language awareness and exposure and less on acquiring a specific language. It is in FLEX programs that issues related to less commonly taught languages are most likely to be, and most easily, addressed in the elementary school context (see Lubiner, 1996; Reagan & Case, 1996).

Last, we come to the contribution that can be made by consideration of the social grammar of the less commonly taught languages to the politics of schooling and to the empowerment and emancipation of both students and teachers. Dell Hymes has argued that, "it is probably through education—taken in its broadest sense, as schooling and instruction of all kinds—that the peculiar, latent, tacit American view of language most powerfully exercises cultural hegemony" (1996, p. 83). It is also, therefore, in educational institutions that we may have the best opportunity to challenge and repudiate this cultural hegemony—to engage, that is, in what Osborn has called "curricular nullification" (1998). This can be done through the inclusion of critical language exploration and awareness programs (see Andrews, 1998; Carter, 1990; van Lier, 1995), in second/foreign language classes themselves, and in other school contexts in which issues of language, power, and domination can be raised (see Fairclough, 1989; Reagan & Osborn, 1998), not to mention contexts in which issues of language rights can be discussed (see Chapter 4). As Michael Byram, Carol Morgan and their colleagues have pointed out in their discussion of language and culture teaching as political education:

> By making comparisons, learners are deliberately led into relativisation of their own perspective through prioritisation of the perspective of others. Comparison is not only a technique for highly similarities and differences as a means of making them more perceptible. It also serves as a step towards the acceptance of other perspectives, and the valuing of them as equally acceptable within their own terms. (1994, p. 177; see also Byram, 1989)

In short, the consideration of the social grammar of the less commonly taught languages provides us with a powerful opportunity to address a broad range of language-related issues in the school context, helping students to become more aware of the nature and role of language in society, language bias and discrimination, and the ways in which language is used and misused with respect to other social, political, and economic issues.

THE LESS COMMONLY TAUGHT LANGUAGES IN THE GLOBAL CONTEXT

The argument presented thus far in this chapter has clearly and explicitly been grounded in and directed toward a U.S. context. However, while the problems with respect to the less commonly taught languages are quite serious in this context, they are by no means unique. Indeed, the same fundamental arguments apply to less commonly taught languages in other societies as well, though of course there will be differences related to local languages of importance in various countries. Thus, while Xhosa is clearly a Level 4 language in the U.S. context, it is a Level 2 language in the South African context (though it may in fact even be moving toward Level 1 status in certain respects). Similarly, the role of Arabic in traditionally Muslim societies will inevitably be quite different than in non-Muslim societies, just as the place of Chinese will be different in Asian societies in which there has been significant cultural and linguistic interaction over the centuries (such as Japan and Korea) than it would be in other societies. Attitudes toward and beliefs about different languages (less commonly taught languages and others) will, then, vary considerably from setting to setting, and this needs to be taken into account in attempting to apply to model provided here in other contexts. For instance, as Brosh has noted with respect to the study of Arabic in Israel, "Arabic is perceived as inherently connected to an ill-esteemed, dangerous, and hostile collective. As a result, the language is perceived as a marker of inferiority, and possessing it could be a source of negative gratification" (1993, p. 355). There is, in short, a strong element of relativism involved in the status of any particular language in different contexts, as of course one would expect.

Most linguists and language educators, I suspect, would share Samuel Johnson's sentiment that, "I am always sorry when any language is lost, because languages are the pedigree of nations" (quoted in Camp, 1990, p. 171). In the case of the less commonly taught languages, we are not dealing so much with the problem of the extinction of languages (although that is, of course, a serious threat to many languages around the world [see Grenoble & Whaley, 1998]) as with a problem of ignorance and apathy. Perhaps even by talking about the less commonly taught languages, then, we can begin to remediate this situation.

NOTES

1. It is important to note that the focus of this chapter is primarily on foreign language education programs, and specifically excludes the use of less commonly taught languages in bilingual programs. The use of less commonly taught languages in bilingual education in the United States, in essence, is transitional in nature, and the primary articulated objective (especially in programs using less commonly taught languages) is the transition of students into English-medium environments. Thus, the fact that the less commonly taught languages may be used in such programs does not in any way detract from the central argument presented here.
2. Although *less commonly taught languages* is the most common term used to describe the languages under discussion here, other terms are sometimes used as well, especially in other countries. Among the more common alternatives are "lesser-used languages" (Grin, 1993) and "minority languages" (C. Williams, 1991).
3. It is interesting to note that of the three commonly taught languages (French, German, and Spanish), two are in Group I (French and Spanish), and one is in Group II (German).

4. The only African language that might, to some extent, count as a Level 3 language in the U.S. context is Swahili.
5. An additional factor which does not appear to be especially relevant in the *contemporary* U.S. context, but which has been important historically in the United States and continues to be so in many societies, is that of ideology (whether religious or political in nature). It is this factor which provides powerful explanatory and heuristic insight, for instance, into the anti-German language hysteria in the United States during the First World War, the role of the development of critical language training in the United States-during the Cold War, and, more recently, some of the concerns among secularists in Turkey to the increased offering of courses in Ottoman Turkish, which is in some instances believed to be symbolically linked to the rise of religious fundamentalism.
6. Along the same lines have been changes in the pedagogy of Latin in recent years. The challenge here has been that the most common approach to the teaching of ancient and classical languages has tended to be, and, with the possible exceptions of Latin and perhaps Classical Greek in some limited instances, continues to be essentially that of grammar translation.
7. An important point to stress here is the difference in educational aims and objectives between bilingual education programs and foreign language programs. This difference is perhaps best seen in terms of the kind of language proficiency that is our goal. In the literature on contemporary U.S. bilingual education, a common distinction is made between what are called "basic interpersonal communicative skills" (BICS) and "cognitive academic language proficiency" (CALP) (see Baker, 2001, pp. 11-12; Spener, 1991, p. 440). The former refers to the language skills needed for casual conversational use of the L2, while the latter refers to the degree and kind of proficiency needed to intellectual and academic purposes. Bilingual educators argue that students achieve BICS far sooner than CALP, and that this distinction makes necessary extended transitional programs for non-English-speaking students in the U.S. context. Although the distinction between BICS and CALP is in fact questionable (see Martin-Jones & Romaine, 1986; Spolsky, 1989), it is an interesting one for discussion purposes here, since the kinds of language proficiency included in BICS probably more than exceed typical expectations for student functioning in the target language in foreign language education programs.

CHAPTER 6

LANGUAGE LEARNING AND FEELINGS OF DISGUST?

The Case of Esperanto[1]

Esperanto. The feeling of disgust we get if we utter an invented word with invented derivative syllables. The word is cold, lacking in associations, and yet it plays at being "language". A system of purely written signs would not disgust us so much.

—*Ludwig Wittgenstein* (1946/1980, p. 53)

Esperanto is a fascinating phenomenon. Not only is it an artificially constructed, planned language, but it is the only such language to have achieved much more than a modicum of success. Its speakers have also been the focus of persecutions in both Nazi German and the Soviet Union under Stalin (see Lins, 1990; Piron, 1989; Sadler & Lins, 1972). Esperanto commonly evokes snickers and even outright laughter among the general public—in one television situation comedy, after a character utters an especially puzzling comment, another member of the cast asks, "What was *that,* Esperanto?" If not quite as amusing as Klingon,[2] Esperanto in short still makes for a good punch line. Second/foreign language educators, however, have often tended to see Esperanto not merely as amusing, but also as something of a challenge and even an affront. This

Critical Questions, Critical Perspectives:
Language and the Second Language Educator, 77–102

reaction is due to a number of factors, not the least of which are the *artificialness* of the language and its supposed ease of acquisition. More than these, though, foreign language educators have been puzzled about why one would choose to learn Esperanto instead of devoting the same time and energy to learning a natural language. In this chapter, I want to provide a broad overview of the origins, nature, structure, and purposes of Esperanto, and then examine the claims that have been made for Esperanto in light of the currently available research evidence. Although the Esperanto movement is indeed somewhat quixotic in nature, there are a number of significant issues surrounding the teaching and learning of Esperanto with which second/foreign language educators ought to be familiar, and from which, perhaps, our own pedagogical practice might benefit (see Goodman, 1978).

WHAT IS ESPERANTO?

Esperanto is a product of post-Enlightenment thought in a variety of ways. From the seventeenth century, there had been numerous efforts to construct artificial languages—initially, for primarily philosophical rather than linguistic purposes (advocated by no less a figure than René Descartes), and later, as attempts to resolve the social and political barriers created by linguistic diversity (see Eco, 1995; Guerard, 1922; Janton, 1993, pp. 1-22; Knowlson, 1975; Stillman, 1995). By the nineteenth century, this second sort of undertaking had become the norm, and by far the most successful of the artificial language projects had been Volapük. Volapük, in spite of its initial successes, failed to survive both its own complexity and the efforts to control its development by its creator, Fr. Johann Martin Schleyer (see Golden, 1997; Guerard, 1922, pp. 96-106). Esperanto was created in the wake of the failure of Volapük by a young Polish Jewish opthalmologist, Lazar Ludwik Zamenhof, in 1887—marked by the publication in Warsaw of a Russian-language pamphlet entitled *La lingvo internacia de Doktoro Esperanto* (*The International Language of Dr. Hopeful*). Zamenhof had grown up in the town of Bialystok, in Russian-occupied Poland. His childhood experiences in this multilingual, multicultural, multinational, multireligious, and deeply divided city led to his concern for the need to unify humanity (see Boulton, 1960). As Zamenhof himself wrote,

> The place where I was born and spent my childhood gave the direction to all my future endeavors. In Bialystok, the population consisted of four diverse elements: Russians, Poles, Germans, and Jews; each spoke a different language and was hostile to the other elements. In this town, more than

> anywhere else, an impressionable nature feels the heavy burden of linguistic differences and is convinced, at every step, that the diversity of languages is the only, or at least the main cause, that separates the human family and divides it into conflicting groups. I was brought up as an idealist; I was taught that all men were brothers, and meanwhile, in the street, in the square, everything at every step made me feel that men did not exist, only Russians, Poles, Germans, Jews and so on. This was always a great torment to my infant mind, although many people may smile at such an "anguish for the world" in a child. Since, at that time, it seemed to me that the grown-ups were omnipotent, I kept telling myself that, when I was grown up, I would certainly destroy this evil. (Quoted in Janton, 1993, p. 24)

For Zamenhof, a successful common language for all humanity would have to meet three necessary conditions (see Nuessel, 2000, pp. 31-32). Such a language would have to be very easy to learn, it would have to have a logical, simple, and regular structure, and there had to be rewards for individuals to learn the language (see Janton, 1993, p. 26). The language that he created, originally called simply the *internacia lingvo* (international language), was intended to meet all of these conditions. It is important to note here that Esperanto was never intended to replace any natural language; rather, the goal was for the language to function as a common second, or auxiliary, language for all people. Thus, bilingualism (in one's mother tongue and in Esperanto) would ensure that every human being would both maintain his or her own language and be able to communicate directly with every other human being. Additionally, because virtually everyone would use Esperanto as a second language, a kind of level playing field would be established, since no one would have the advantage in multilingual settings of using their own native language. The language that Ludwik Zamenhof created, although by no means succeeding in its broad objective of becoming a shared universal language, nevertheless survived and even, to some extent, thrived over the course of the twentieth century—in spite of becoming a target for suspicion and even oppression in many societies. Although estimates vary considerably (from tens of millions to the more common figure of 1,000,000) (see D. Richardson, 1988, p. 18), and are exceptionally difficult to evaluate critically, at the start of the twenty-first century, there are very conservatively at least 120,000 fluent speakers of Esperanto in the world, and hundreds of thousands of others who have at least a passing knowledge of the language (see Nuessel, 2000, p. 24; though Gledhill, 2000, p. 10, provides an even lower estimate of 40,000 truly fluent speakers). In any event, what is clear is that Esperanto, compared to all other efforts to create artificial or planned languages, has been remarkably successful. As Pierre Janton has noted,

> "All theoretical argument is beside the point: Esperanto already works," affirmed the well-known linguist Antoine Meillet in 1928. Hundreds of thousands of Esperantists have proved him right. Anonymous students in night classes or scholars of work repute, together they have vitalized the movement through their dedication and idealism.... Over the past century, the idea and project of a single idealistic individual, Lazer Ludwik Zamenhof, has extended across the continents as a multifaceted, pluralistic, but united diaspora, a harbinger of that world order of which Zamenhof dreamed. Unlike other planned languages, Esperanto emerged from its intellectual and social birthplace and established itself among the modest but hardworking and thoughtful elements of society that have defended it obstinately and generously over the years. (Janton, 1993, p. 129)

Although it is indeed difficult, if not impossible, to estimate the number of speakers of Esperanto, it is considerably easier to observe its status and use in the contemporary world. As D. Richardson notes,

> Taken worldwide, the Esperanto movement these days is a far-flung but close-knit network of mostly independent bodies. Local, national, and international organizations, as well as specialized societies, book and magazine publishers, and even a few special-interest groups work side-by-side to further the language and its usefulness. Among these disparate bodies there is considerable cooperation, but little hegemony: rarely does one group have any real authority over another. (1988, p. 45)

The Esperanto movement is united in part by the Universala Esperanto-Asocio (Universal Esperanto Association), as well as by various local and national organizations. There are a wide array of publications (books, journals, magazines, and newspapers) available in Esperanto, including both translated materials and original publications written in Esperanto. There are annual World Esperanto Congresses, as well as a voluntary travel service, the Delegita Servo (actually, more of a system of local representatives), and speciality organizations representing religious groups, sports groups, cultural groups, and so on. In short, there is a well-established and effectively functioning international Esperanto speech community (although perhaps it may be more accurate to call it a *speech network*).[3] Esperanto has also been the focus of a good deal of linguistic research (see Tonkin & Fettes, 1996; R. Wood, 1982), especially in the area of interlinguistics (see Duliĉenko, 1988, 1989; Fettes, 2001, 2003a, 2003b; Tonkin, 1997).

THE STRUCTURE OF ESPERANTO

In order to understand many of the claims made about the teaching and learning of Esperanto, it is necessary to have at least a passing acquaintance with the structure of the language (see Moore, 1980). Although it is obviously neither appropriate nor possible to provide a complete linguistic analysis of Esperanto here, it may be helpful to provide a broad overview of its structure.

The core of Esperanto grammar is provided in Zamenhof's Sixteen Rules, which provide a basic scaffolding for the language (see Appendix A). Although the Sixteen Rules are certainly basic to the language, they provide an incomplete description of the grammar of the language (Nuessel, 2000, p. 24), as Janton has explained:

> Fundamental though they may be, these rules alone cannot describe the language adequately. Esperanto cannot be reduced to such a skeletal structure: like all living languages, it has its own complex autonomy. Accordingly, we must apply to it the same methods of investigation as we would use for any living language. (1993, p. 44)

We therefore turn now to a brief linguistic overview of Esperanto, focusing on the phonological and morphological characteristics of the language.

Phonologically, Esperanto is clearly based on the Indo-European languages with which Zamenhof was personally familiar. Both phonologically and lexically, the languages from which Esperanto draws its norms include Yiddish, Hebrew, Polish, Russian, French, English, German, Lithuanian, Latin, and Greek. The phonology of Esperanto is fairly straightforward, as one would expect from a language designed to be both simple and regular (see Kalocsay & Waringhien, 1985, pp. 39-49). There is, however, a certain degree of diversity in the pronunciation of Esperanto, in part due to interference from the native language of the individual speaker (Janton, 1993, p. 47; Wells, 1989, pp. 17-26), and in part caused by changes within the Esperanto speech community itself (see Gledhill, 2000, p. 17; Kuznetsov, 1988; Lo Jacomo, 1981). The cardinal vowel system of Esperanto is generally presented in Table 6.1 (see Kuznetsov, 1988, p. 39; Gledhill, 2000, p. 19; Nuessel, 2000, p. 42; Wells, 1989, p. 18).

A variant of this cardinal vowel system, also documented in the literature (see Janton, 1993, p. 47; Nuessel, 2000, p. 42), is presented in Table 6.2.

Table 6.1. Esperanto Cardinal Vowel System

	Front	*Central*	*Back*
High	i		u
Mid	e		o
Low		a	

Table 6.2. Variant of Esperanto Cardinal Vowel System

	Front	*Central*	*Back*
High	i		u
Mid	ɛ		ɔ
Low		a	

Table 6.3. Esperanto Consonantal System

Consonants	*Bilabial*	*Labio-Dental*	*Dental*	*Post-Alveolar*	*Palatal*	*Velar*	*Glottal*
Stop (-voice)	/p/		/t/			/k/	
Stop (+voice)	/b/		/d/			/g/	
Affricate (-voice)			/s/	/tʃ/			
Affricate (+voice)			/z/	/dʒ/			
Fricative (-voice)		/f/	/ts/	/ʃ/		/x/	/h/
Fricative (+voice)		/v/		/ʒ/			
Nasal	/m/		/n/				
Lateral				/l/			
Uvular Roll				/r/			
Semi-Vowels	/w/				/j/		

In addition, Esperanto has six descending dipthongs (*aj* /ai/, *ej* /ɛi/, *oj* *ɔi*/, *uj* /ui/, *aŭ* /au/, and *eŭ* /ɛu/), and two glides (i.e., semi-vowels), *ŭ* and *j* (the latter pronounced like "y" in English). The complete consonantal system of Esperanto is presented in Table 6.3 (see Gledhill, 2000, p. 19).

Accent in Esperanto is fixed and regular, and falls on the penultimate syllable of the word (e.g., *hómo* "man," *árbo* "tree," *língvo* "language," *Esperánto,* etc.). Orthographically, Esperanto "constitutes an almost perfect phonological representation of the system of phonemes because each grapheme represents a single phoneme" (Janton, 1993, p. 46). The Esperanto alphabet, which does contain some letters not found in English, can be found in Appendix B.

The lexicon of Esperanto is perhaps the most *mixed* aspect of the language, although this is to some extent an understatement, as Christopher Gledhill has explained:

> Esperanto's vocabulary is usually described as a mix of words from Latin, French and other European languages. The picture is much more complicated than this, however. Zamenhof also equipped the language with a stock of grammatical words which resembled no one language in particular. More importantly, despite originating from one or another language, the majority of words in Esperanto were modified and accommodated into a more neutral form.... In addition, the basic morphological rules of Esperanto inevitably led to word forms that were unique to the language. (2000, p. 20)

The Esperanto lexicon includes words derived from Romance languages (especially French and Latin), Germanic languages (primarily German, Yiddish, and English), Balto-Slavic languages (especially Russian, Serbo-Croatian, and Polish, as well as Lithuanian), Greek, from shared Indo-European roots, and finally, small numbers of lexical items from Hebrew, Arabic, Japanese, Chinese, and other languages (see Gledhill, 2000, pp. 20-26; Janton, 1993, pp. 51-55). Estimates of the distribution of the lexicon by source language vary somewhat, but it is likely that between 70% and 75% of the lexical items in Esperanto are Romance in origin, and 10% to 20% are Germanic in origin. Kolker (1988) has suggested a much more significant impact of Russian on the Esperanto lexicon, while Gold (1980, 1982) has examined the influence of both Hebrew and Yiddish on Esperanto (see also Piron, 1984).

Among the more interesting elements of Esperanto is its morphology (see Hana, 1998; Kalocsay & Waringhien, 1985, pp. 53-177). Typologically, Esperanto is essentially an agglutinative language (Wells, 1989, pp. 33-34), although some linguists have argued that such a classification is at best incomplete, since Esperanto also demonstrates a number of important nonagglutinating linguistic aspects, "including the freedom of word derivation and monomorphism that are reminiscent of isolating languages" (Gledhill, 2000, p. 40; see also Piron, 1991), and others have identified elements of inflecting or fusional languages in Esperanto's morphology (see Kalocsay, 1931/1963).

The verbal morphology of Esperanto is characterized first by an absolutely regular tense, voice and aspect system. The infinitive form of all verbs in Esperanto ends in *-i;* this ending is replaced with other suffixes to indicate tense (*-as* for present tense, *-is* for past tense, and *-os* for future tense). The verb is uninflected for person, thus:

paroli	infinitive	to speak
mi parolas	present tense	I speak, I am speaking

vi parolas		you (sing./pl.) speak, you are speaking
li parolas		he speaks, he is speaking
ni parolas		we speak, we are speaking
ili parolas		they speak, they are speaking
mi parolis	past tense	I spoke
etc.		
mi parolos	future tense	I will speak
etc.		

The conditional is formed by adding the suffix *-us* (*mi parolus,* "I would speak"), and the imperative by adding *-u* (*Parolu!* "Speak!"). Participles distinguish both between active and passive voice and between perfective and nonperfective aspect:

parolanto	active, nonperfective	[a person] in the act of speaking
parolonto	active, nonperfective	[a person] about to speak
parolinto	active, perfective	having spoken
parolato	passive, nonperfective	in the process of being spoken about
paroloto	passive, nonperfective	about to be spoken of
parolito	passive, nonperfective	having been spoken about

Esperanto's verbal morphology is also characterized by a systemic approach to verbal transformations utilizing affixes to change the meaning of a base verb. The affixes most commonly used include: *ek-* (to begin), *-ad-* (a prolonged or continual action), *-ig-* (causative), and *-iĝ-* (a change of state). Thus, from the infinitive *trinki* (to drink), one can produce:

trinki	to drink
ektrinki	to begin to drink
trinkigi	to cause to drink
trinkĝi	to be being drunk[4]
trinkadi	to continue to drink
ektrinkigi	to cause (someone) to begin to drink
trinkiĝigi	to make (someone/thing to be) drunk
trinkigadi	to continue to cause (someone) to drink
trinkadigi	to cause (someone) to continue to drink
trinkiĝadi	to keep (someone/thing) being drunk

To some extent, though, it needs to be noted that some of these forms are more theoretically possible than real in actual Esperanto language use. As Humphrey Tonkin has observed,

> The key point that I would make ... is that Esperanto is first and foremost a spoken and written language, with a whole host of nonce usages, slang, verbal play, etc., that [such] analyses ... don't even begin to capture. Thus, for example, there is no conditional participle in Esperanto, say the grammarians, and yet you hear words like *"parolunto"* (someone who may or may not talk, or someone who would have talked if he had been given half a chance) all the time. *"Alia"*, other, is not a correlative, so how do you account for *"alies"* (someone else's)—a term widely used by not regarded as "proper" Esperanto? (personal communication, July 15, 2004)

This point is well taken, and indeed is supported by recent empirical research on the process of overregularization of grammatical forms in Esperanto by native speaking children (see Corsetti, Pinto, & Tolomeo, 2004).

The nominal and adjectival morphology of Esperanto are similarly productive. Esperanto nouns and adjectives show number as well as case (nominative and objective). For nouns, the endings are as follows:

Nouns	Singular	Plural
Nominative	*-o*	*-oj*
Objective	*-on*	*-ojn*

For adjectives, the endings are:

Adjectives	Singular	Plural
Nominative	*-a*	*-aj*
Objective	*-an*	*-ajn*

Thus,

La bona libro estas sur la tablo.	The good book is on the table.
La bonaj libroj estas sur la tablo.	The good books are on the table.
Mi havas bonan libron.	I have a good book.
Vi aĉetis du bonajn librojn.	You bought two good books.

In addition, there are a number of common affixes used with nouns (and in some cases with adjectives and adverbs) in Esperanto to change lexical meaning. Table 6.4 provides a list of such affixes, an indication of the meaning of each affix, and an example of each (see Jordan, 1992, pp. 101-131, and Conroy, 1994, pp. 341-342, from which much of Table 6.4 is derived).

Finally, one of the more interesting aspects of Esperanto morphology is the system of correlatives. Basically, the correlatives are relative pronouns and quantifiers, which "serve an adjectival or an adverbial function, as

Table 6.4. Common Affixes in Esperanto

Affix	*Meaning*	*Example*
bo-	attached to a kinship term to indicate an in-law relationship	*frato* "brother" *bofrato* "brother-in-law"
dis-	dispersion in all directions	*rompi* "to break" *disrompi* "to smash to pieces"
eks-	cognate to English -ex (meaning "former")	*edzino* "wife" *eksedzino* "ex-wife"
fi-	indicates that the root refers to something of low moral quality	*libro* "book" *filibro* "dirty book"
ge-	indicates that both males and females are included	*fratoj* "brothers" *gefratoj* "siblings"
mal-	indicates the reverse of the meaning of the root word; widely used with adjectives and adverbs	*bona* "good" *malbona* "bad"
ne-	indicates the negation of the meaning of the root word	*sincera* "sincere" *nesincera* "insincere"
mis-	indicates the malfunction of whatever is suggested by the root word	*kompreni* "to understand" *miskompreni* "to misunderstand"
pra-	indicates great antiquity	*historio* "history" *prahistorio* "prehistory"
re-	indicates either repetition or a return to a previous state or condition	*doni* "to give" *redoni* "to give back"
-a ĉ -	indicates disparagement; expresses the idea that the root is of poor quality	*vesto* "clothing" *vesta ĉ o* "rags worn as clothing"
-a ĵ-	indicates a concrete object or product associated with the root word	*trinki* "to drink" *trinka ĵ o* " a drink"
-an-	indicates a member of a group or membership in a group (including nationality, religion, etc.)	*Kristo* "Christ" *kristano* "Christian" klubana
-ar-	indicates a group of whatever is indicated by the root word	*profesoro* "professor" *profesoraro* "faculty"
-ĉ j-	used to form nicknames for males (cf. *-nj-* for females)	*patro* "father" *patr ĉ jo* "daddy" (Note that these suffixes, unlike the others, involve substitution for part of the root word.)
-ebl-	indicates possibility (usually used with a transitive verb)	*man ĝ i* "to eat" man ĝ ebla "edible"
-ec-	indicates an abstract quality associated with the root word	*bela* "beautiful" *beleco* "beauty"

(Table continues on next page)

Table 6.4. Continued

Affix	*Meaning*	*Example*
-eg-	increases the size or strength of the root word (cf. *-et-*)	*domo* " house" *domego* "mansion"
-ej-	refers to a place	*lerni* "to learn" *lernejo* "school"
-em-	indicates a tendency toward what the root word expresses	*ami* "to love" *amema* "amorous"
-end-	indicates necessity	*vidi* "to see" *videnda* "which must be seen"
-er-	indicates a single element of the root word	*pluvo* "rain" *pluvero* "raindrop"
-estr-	indicates the "chief" or "boss" of whatever is suggested by the root word	*lernejo* "school" *lernejestro* "principal"
-foj-	attached to nouns to indicate "times"	*tri* "three" *trifoje* "three times, thrice"
-et-	decreases the size or strength of the root word (cf. *-eg-*)	*domo* " house" *dometo* "cottage"
-id-	indicates offspring of the root word	*kato* "cat" *katido* "kitten"
-il-	indicates an instrument used to perform the function of the root word	*kombi* "to comb" *kombilo* "a comb"
-in-	indicates female	*knabo* "child, boy" *knabino* "girl"
-nj-	used to form nicknames for females (cf. *-ĉj-* for males)	*patrino* "mother" *panjo* "mommy"
-ind-	indicates worthiness, or worthy of the root word	*fari* "to do" *farinda* "worth doing"
-ism-	cognate to English -ism (referring to a philosophy, ideology, or movement)	*internacia* "international" *internaciismo* "internationalism"
-ist-	refers to a person	*instrui* "to teach, instruct" *instruisto* "teacher"
-obl-	indicates the multiplication of the quantity expressed by the root word	*du* "two" *duobla* "double"
-on-	added to a number to indicate a fraction	*du* "two" *duono* "one-half"
-op-	added to numbers to indicate "at a time"	*tri* "three" *triope* "in threes"
-uj- / *-ing-*	indicate containers for the root word (*-uj-* is a container for several of whatever the root word is, while *-ing-* is a container for at most one of whatever the root word is)	*ovo* "egg" *ovujo* "egg carton" *ovingo* "egg cup"

(Table continues on next page)

Table 6.4. Continued

Affix	*Meaning*	*Example*
-ul-	indicates a person characterized by the root word	*alta* "tall" *altulo* "a tall person"
-um-	this is used primarily with nouns to form derivatives where no other affix is appropriate	*kruco* "cross" *krucumi* "to crucify" *buterumi* "to spread butter on something" *okulumi* "to make eyes at someone" *foliumi (libron)* "to leaf through a book"

well as a nominal and pronominal function" (Nuessel, 2000, p. 50). The correlative system is an extremely efficient way of conveying an immense amount of both grammatical and semantic information. Basically, the system involves nine series of five morphemes, which indicate different correlative functions. As Janton explains, "the first morpheme in each series is simple and indefinite, and the other four are derived from it with the aid of a particular initial consonant" (1993, p. 59). Thus, there are two sets of correlatives,[5] as presented in Table 6.5 (based on Janton, 1993, pp. 59-60).

Taken as a whole, the morphology of Esperanto is thus impressively regular and predictable, and allows the learner to master a great deal of morphological, lexical and syntactic information relatively quickly and easily, which of course has been one of the more common arguments used by advocates of Esperanto in promoting the language, as we shall see in the following section of the chapter.

THE EDUCATIONAL CLAIMS MADE FOR ESPERANTO

Advocates and proponents of Esperanto, inspired by their enthusiasm for both the language and the movement with which it is affiliated, have over the years made numerous claims about the educational, social, and political advantages of Esperanto (see, for example, Esperanto League for North American and the California Esperanto Education Commission, 1988; Fantini & Reagan, 1992; Glossop, 1988, 1991; Leon-Smith, 1987; Markarian, 1964; Maxwell, 1988; Nuessel, 2000, pp. 59-66; Sherwood, 1982a, 1982b, 1983; Symoens, 1989). These claims have been supported by a combination of common sense, logic, anecdotal evidence, and a limited but growing number of empirical studies. Typical in this regard is Richardson's assertion that:

Table 6.5. Esperanto System of Corralatives

Pronominal-Adjectival Correlatives

	Individual	*Quality*	*Thing*	*Possessor*
Indefinite	*iu* "someone, somebody, some"	*ia* "some kind of"	*io* "something"	*ies* "someone"s, something"s"
Interrogative	*kiu* "who, what"	*kia* "what kind of"	*kio* "what"	*kies* "whose"
Demonstrative	*tiu* "that person, that"	*tia* "that kind of"	*tio* "that thing"	*ties* "that person"s, that thing"s"
Collective	*ĉ iu* "everyone, everybody, every"	*ĉ ia* "every kind of"	*ĉ io* "everything"	*ĉ ies* "everyone"s, everything"s"
Negative	*neniu* "no one, nobody"	*nenia* "no kind of"	*nenio* "nothing"	*nenies* "no one"s, nothing"s"

Adverbial Correlatives

	Quantity	*Place*	*Time*	*Cause*	*Manner*
Indefinite	*iom* "some, some amount, somewhat"	*ie* "somewhere"	*iam* "sometime"	*ial* "for some reason"	*iel* "in some way, somehow"
Interrogative	*kiom* "how much, how many"	*kie* "where"	*kiam* "when, at what time"	*kial* "why, for what reason"	*kiel* "in what way, how"
Demonstrative	*tiom* "that much, that many, so much, so many"	*tie* "there"	*tiam* "at that time, then"	*tial* "for that reason, therefore, so"	*tiel* "in that way, thus"
Collective	*ĉ iom* "the whole quantity, all of it"	*ĉ ie* "everywhere"	*ĉ iam* "always, every time"	*ĉ ial* "for all reasons, for every reason"	*ĉ iel* "in all ways, in every way"
Negative	*neniom* "none, no amount"	*nenie* "nowhere"	*neniam* "never"	*nenial* "for no reason"	*neniel* "in no way"

Then again, Esperanto's potential value to education could prove decisive. We have seen how teaching Esperanto in elementary and high-school classes results in better understanding of how languages work, promotes language skills generally, and can lead to more (and more effective) foreign-

> language study besides. Schools that cannot afford full-blown foreign language programs can afford to teach Esperanto, and with superior results in the long run. (1988, p. 62)

In the remainder of this chapter, an effort will be made to clarify the educational claims that have been made by supporters of Esperanto, and then to examine and evaluate the evidence available with respect to each claim. It is important to note here that there are a variety of other kinds of claims made on behalf of Esperanto (such as its economic benefits in international organizations, its role in promoting linguistic equality, and so on [see Auld, 1988; Dodge, 1941; Jordan, 1997; Pool, 1987; Tonkin, 1988]) that are beyond the scope of this discussion.

Esperantists have advocated the teaching and learning of Esperanto as a common, second international language since its creation in the nineteenth century. Indeed, to a very great extent the need to promote the teaching and learning of Esperanto is a central component of the language's *raison d'être* (see Fisher, 1921; Forster, 1982; Gregor, 1976; Guerard, 1922; Janton, 1988; Large, 1985; Nuessel, 2000), although the Esperanto movement is obviously far more than merely a language movement. As Peter Forster has noted with respect to the Esperanto movement in Britain, "many of its [Esperanto's] supporters make much wider claims for Esperanto. A quasi-religious fervour is often associated with the language, and Esperanto is frequently linked by its speakers with the cause of world peace" (1982, p. 3).

In their efforts to promote Esperanto, the supporters of the language have offered a wide range of arguments to encourage others to consider both personal and (of greater importance here) public commitments to the language. Among the more important social and political claims that have been made about Esperanto by its advocates are the following:

- Esperanto is easier, and faster, to learn than are national/ethnic languages. This claim is most commonly manifested in comparisons of the learning time involved in acquiring competence in Esperanto with that needed for a national/ethnic language, although the regularity of Esperanto's structure is also often used to support the claim that it is easier to acquire than a national/ethnic language.
- Esperanto, because of its logical and a priori nature, can be taught more efficiently and explicitly than can national/ethnic languages. The basic idea here is that while national/ethnic languages are generally best taught inductively, this is not necessarily the case with Esperanto, and, further, that direct, explicit instruction will make both teaching and learning more efficient. The fundamental idea here is that because Esperanto strives to avoid the irregularities,

inconsistencies, and complexities of national/ethnic languages (while at the same time preserving the fullest possible degree of linguistic expression), several assumptions are commonly made about its learnability. Specifically, it is often assumed that (a) Esperanto is more learnable (that is, that any given level of proficiency can be achieved in Esperanto with less effort and in shorter time than with any national/ethnic language) and (b) that its superiority in terms of learnability is much greater than any inherent biases in its vocabulary or structure that would favor speakers of some languages (for example, speakers of Indo-European languages) over others.

- The learning of Esperanto has propaedeutic effects with respect to the learning of other languages, and perhaps even other subject matter. In other words, the learning of Esperanto will reduce the time needed for the learning of other languages (and perhaps other subject matter, such as geography, mathematics, etc.). As an investment, in short, learning Esperanto may have significant benefits unrelated to the acquisition of the international language itself.
- The learning of Esperanto has positive benefits for students' knowledge and understanding of their own language, as well as of language in general. The argument here is essentially the same as that offered for second/foreign language study in general: in many cases, students learn the basic concepts of grammar as these relate to their own language through the study of other languages.
- The learning of Esperanto has a positive effect on students' self-confidence. As a result of successful learning of Esperanto, students will feel more competent and empowered, and this will result in a higher level of self-confidence (which, in turn, can result in improved learning in other areas).
- The learning of Esperanto offers an effective way of countering ethnocentrism and encouraging an attitude of toleration of cultural differences in students. An important theme in schooling in a growing number of societies, and especially in the United States, during the last 2 decades has been the concern with the promotion of multicultural education and the concomitant concern with reducing ethnocentrism. It has been suggested that learning Esperanto will have a positive effect with respect to these goals.
- The learning of Esperanto facilitates the development of a more global perspective, and provides access to an international cultural community. Especially common in this regard are claims related to the use of international correspondence, pen pals, and so on.

- Learning Esperanto is especially appropriate for students with special needs (including both gifted/talented students and those with learning disabilities). Although different arguments are used, claims have been made that students at both extremes of the population may have greater interest in and success with Esperanto than with other types of subject matter (see, e.g., Quick, 1989; R. Wood, 1975).
- The learning of Esperanto will encourage students to learn other languages. This claim is essentially the affective counterpart to the claim about the propaedeutic effects of learning Esperanto: not only will the study of Esperanto have a positive effect on the acquisition of other languages, but by studying Esperanto, students will also be more likely to wish to study additional languages.

Taken as a whole, these claimed benefits are quite impressive, if indeed they turn out to be true. We turn now to an examination and evaluation of the existing research base on the teaching and learning of Esperanto, in an effort to determine the extent to which each of these claims is supported by the empirical evidence currently available.

THE RESEARCH BASE

The empirical evidence that constitutes the core of the research base with respect to the teaching and learning of Esperanto has been summarized in several places (see Fantini & Reagan, 1992; Markarian, 1964; Maxwell, 1988; Symoens, 1989; Tonkin, 1977; R. Wood, 1975), and while all of these summaries are now somewhat dated, the picture that they present remains fairly accurate. For our purposes here, four major research undertakings will be discussed and evaluated. Specifically, we will examine the findings of the studies conducted by the Institute of Educational Research at Teachers College, Columbia University (1924 to 1935), the studies conducted at Denton Grammar School in Britain, the two "five-country" experiments conducted under the supervision of Istvan Szerdahelyi (from 1971 to 1974 in the first region and from 1971 to 1977 in the second region), and the ongoing research conducted by the Instituto pri Kibernetika Pedagogio at the University of Paderborn, Germany.

The Teachers College Study

The Teachers College study actually consists of three related experimental studies, taking place in 1924, 1928 to 1931, and 1934-1935, respectively (see Division of Psychology, 1933). Directed and supervised by the well-known educational psychologist Edward L. Thorndike, and involving the assistance of Drs. Laura Kennon and Helen Eaton, the Teachers College Study at Columbia University focused on such issues as the learnability of auxiliary languages in general (and Esperanto in particular), as well as on the propaedeutic effects of Esperanto study on future language learning. Involving subjects ranging in age from 8 to 65, in a variety of different types of classroom settings, the Teachers College Study results indicated that, given the same amount of exposure, students will learn more Esperanto than they would of a national/ethnic language. In fact, the 1933 report included the claim that, "an average college senior or graduate in twenty hours of study will be able to understand printed and spoken Esperanto better than he understands French or German or Italian or Spanish after a hundred hours of study" (Division of Psychology, 1933, pp. 6-7). This assertion appears to be the basis for the common assertion that Esperanto is roughly five times easier to learn than a national/ethnic language. The report, in fact, actually made an even stronger claim, noting that "on the whole, with expenditures of from ten to a hundred hours, the achievement in the synthetic language will probably be from five to fifteen times that in a natural language, according to the difficulty of the latter" (Division of Psychology, 1933, p. 7).

The empirical foundation for these claims, however, is weak at best, being based on very limited test results that did not adequately take into account compounding variables. However, the general claim that Esperanto is easier to learn than a national/ethnic language—a claim that can offer in its defense both common sense and impressive anecdotal evidence—does receive reasonably compelling support from the Teachers College Study. As the 1933 report notes, "two facts are certain. Any one of the reputable 'synthetic' languages is very much easier to learn than any natural language; but its learning is none the less a very substantial task" (Division of Psychology, 1933, p. 6).

As for the propaedeutic effects of Esperanto study, the Teachers College did suggest that there were positive outcomes associated with the study of Esperanto for both English and French learning. The report summarizes the results as follows:

> So at the end of two years the English scores are more or less the same, though slightly higher for the Esperanto group; the French scores show 9.7 points more progress for the Esperanto group, which had studied French during one of the two years, than was made by the non-Esperanto group, which had studied French during the two years. (Division of Psychology, 1933, p. 30)

While these results do appear to be impressive, it should be kept in mind that they were based on a very small sample, and that the study did not involve carefully maintained experimental and control groups. In fact, the authors of the report themselves were clearly very hesitant to draw any substantial conclusions from their data. At best, as far as the propaedeutic effects of Esperanto study are concerned, the Teachers College study is marginally supportive of the positive claims that are often made.

The Denton Grammar School Study

The Denton Grammar School was the site of a 25-year study of the propaedeutic effects of Esperanto study, conducted by the school's headmaster, Norman Williams. In the midst of this 25-year period, from 1947 through 1951, a more limited 4-year study was conducted by a specialist from Sheffield University (Halloran, 1952). The results of both N. Williams (1965) and Halloran (1952) were, on the whole, supportive of the claim that Esperanto study has a positive effect on further language study, though Halloran did find that more academically gifted students tested slightly better in French if they had 4 years of French instruction rather than a year of Esperanto followed by 3 years of French. N. Williams (1965) argued, however, that Halloran's approach was actually biased against the Esperanto group, and that no students were disadvantaged by taking Esperanto first. Halloran and Williams both found that academically less able students benefited from initial Esperanto instruction. Although a number of methodological problems and limitations in the studies of Halloran and Williams can be raised, it would appear that their results are for the most part reasonable representations of the Denton experience, and would tend to support the claims for the propaedeutic effects of Esperanto study, as well as those concerned with the positive effects of Esperanto study for special needs students.

The "Five-Country" Experiments

The first of the two five-country experiments, which took place between 1971 and 1974, was conducted in central and eastern Europe (the five countries involved were Hungary, Bulgaria, Italy, and Serbia and Slovenia in Yugoslavia) under the supervision of Istvan Szerdahelyi, Professor of Esperanto and Interlinguistics at the Eötvös Loránd University in Budapest. The primary objective of this study was to determine the relative effectiveness and ease of teaching Esperanto. A total of nearly 1,000 students in some 32 schools were taught Esperanto as their first foreign language, utilizing a common textbook, over a 3-year period. Testing was conducted at the end of the first and second years of the experiment to compare the success of the Esperanto groups with comparable groups studying English, Russian, German, and Italian, and the results, which Szerdahelyi evaluated in terms of what he called "success coefficients," were generally favorable to the Esperanto group (Szerdahelyi, 1975). In other words, in a comparable classroom setting students are likely to learn more Esperanto than they would a national/ethnic language. No testing was conducted at the end of the third year, but, as Wood notes,

> [Students'] competence in the language was thereafter subjected to a practical test when 85 of the participants, *not* selected for their academic success ... attended a vacation school program in the most centrally located and politically neutral participating country, Yugoslavia, at the resort of Primosten, where the organized Esperanto movement holds regular cultural and recreational events. At Primosten the students of diverse language backgrounds continued to be taught, jointly, in [Esperanto], which is the vehicle for all communication at the vacation camp. They studied and played together in it. An international pedagogical Board of Visitors, numbering seven, observed the experiment, noting the use of [Esperanto] in the classroom and play settings, and conversing in Esperanto with the children. (R. Wood, 1975, p. 64)

While this experiment is often cited as evidence of the effectiveness of Esperanto learning, it is unfortunately quite limited in its value. The test results from the first 2 years of the experiment involve a large number of variables which do not seem to have been controlled for (including a lack of control groups from both Bulgaria and Italy, significant variations in actual amount of classroom language instruction as well as classroom size, variations in teacher training and competence, and so on). Further, although Szerdahelyi's use of success coefficients is both creative and intriguing, it is by no means the only way to analyze the data (see, e.g., Maxwell, 1988; Szerdahelyi & Frank, 1976). As for the culminating experience in year three of the study, while the Primosten experience appears to have been successful, its research value is essentially comparable to that of other anecdotal evidence. In short, the most reasonable conclusion to draw from the first of the five-country experiments is that Esperanto can be taught in the classroom setting in ways comparable to the teaching of other languages, and that students may learn Esperanto somewhat more rapidly than national/ethnic languages. Any claims beyond this general conclusion do not appear to be supported by the evidence of the study.

The second of the five-country experiments took place between 1975 and 1977, and involved students in France, Belgium, West Germany, Greece, and the Netherlands (see Sonnabend, 1979). The results of the tests conducted during this study were strongly supportive of claims about the ease and speed of learning Esperanto. However, only for the German classes were control groups included in the study, so these results are, again, less compelling than they might otherwise have been. The evidence on the German classes, though, is quite powerful, as Maxwell notes in his critique of the study:

> Children learning Esperanto were able to learn more in two years than other children learning English in three or four years ... the Esperanto groups would require a total of 2.5 years to obtain 100% mastery of the material presented in this test, whereas the English groups would require 5.3 years to achieve a corresponding result. (Maxwell, 1988, p. 58)

This is especially impressive when one takes into account the fact that the Esperanto group were 3 to 4 years younger than the English group—thus, the Esperanto students learned more, faster, and at an earlier age.

The Paderborn Studies

The Instituto pri Kibernetika Pedagogio (Institute for Cybernetic Pedagogy) at the University of Paderborn, under the leadership of Professor Helmar Frank, has been one of the more productive centers for research on the teaching and learning of Esperanto. Much of the work of the Instituto pri Kibernetika Pedagogio has focused on the relative ease of learning Esperanto in contrast with national/ethnic languages, as well as on the role of Esperanto in promoting language awareness and the propaedeutic effects of Esperanto on the study of national/ethnic languages (see Frank, 1978, 1987a, 1987b; Frank & Barandovska, 1991; Geisler, 1979; Meder, 1978; Meinhardt, 1978). The results obtained by the researchers at the Instituto pri Kibernetika Pedagogio are of quite high quality, and generally appear to support both claims about the ease of learnability of Esperanto and claims about its propaedeutic benefits. Perhaps most interesting publications of the Instituto pri Kibernetika Pedagogio have been Professor Frank's work on the development of a cybernetic-pedagogical representation of the relative propaedeutic benefits of Esperanto (see Frank, 1987a, 1987b).

DISCUSSION AND EVALUATION OF THE RESEARCH

In evaluating the research evidence offered in support of the claims offered by advocates of Esperanto, a number of general factors need to be kept in mind. The research literature that is available to us for evaluating these claims is problematic in a number of ways. First, although a small body of empirical research has been conducted (specifically, Division of

Psychology, 1933; Frank, 1976, 1987a, 1987b; Frank & Barandovska, 1991; Szerdahelyi, 1966, 1975; Szerdahelyi & Frank, 1976), the greatest support for the claims made by Esperantists tends to be anecdotal and personal in nature. Second, the empirical studies that have been conducted to date, with few exceptions, suffer from various methodological limitations that weaken their validity and thus their conclusions (see, for example, Maxwell, 1988). Third, the studies suffer from a weakness common to the literature on Esperanto in general: they have been conducted and written *by* insiders largely *for* insiders (see Jane Edwards, 1986). In essence, the research on the teaching and learning of Esperanto has been, for the most part, separate from that concerned with second/foreign language teaching and learning in general, and as a result has not been subjected to normal academic discussion and evaluation. As Forster has argued with respect to linguistic studies of Esperanto,

> there is no clear consensus among linguists about the matter. Yet in many areas of academic life, where there is no clear consensus a lively debate on the subject ensues. This does not seem to happen very much in the case of Esperanto. Esperanto might merit the occasional paragraph in a book or mention in a lecture, but there is little serious investigation. (Forster, 1987, p. 208)

Markarian has also discussed this problem, noting in the context of a 1963 international report on the teaching of second/foreign languages in primary education that, "the educational role of an international language is never at any point discussed. It is not discussed and rejected: it is not even discussed" (1964, p. 4). This problem has been further exacerbated by the fact that much of the literature concerned with reporting studies on the teaching and learning of Esperanto is available only in Esperanto, thus making the research literature inaccessible to many potential, but non-Esperanto-speaking, supporters. Finally, much of the actual research on the teaching and learning of Esperanto has been conducted in Europe, and often in eastern Europe (the only major empirical study conducted in the U.S. context is that done by the Institute of Educational Research at Teachers College, Columbia University, in the 1920s and 1930s [see Division of Psychology, 1933]). While these studies may be of very high quality, and may offer fascinating insights and what seems to insiders to be compelling evidence, their cultural and geographic distance from the North American context makes them suspect from the perspective of many American educators and policymakers. Taken together, these factors severely limit the usefulness of the research base on the teaching and learning of Esperanto. However, this is not by any means to suggest that nothing can be learned from this research base. On the contrary, we can learn a great deal from earlier work, and the evaluation of such work can provide us with valuable information and insights about where further research would be most useful.

Based on the research that has been conducted thus far on the teaching and learning of Esperanto, a number of conclusions can be drawn with reasonable certainty. The empirical evidence, though far from incontrovertible, is generally in accord with anecdotal evidence with respect to claims about the ease of learnability of Esperanto, its propaedeutic effects on learning additional languages, its use in teaching students about the nature of language in general, and its positive affective benefits for students.

Claims for which there does not appear to be substantial, clear empirical evidence include the claim that the study of Esperanto will increase students' knowledge of and aptitude in their own native language, that the study of Esperanto will result in a countering of ethnocentrism and the development of an attitude of tolerance on the part of students, that there may be nonlanguage related propaedeutic effects from the study of Esperanto, that the study of Esperanto will result in a more global perspective on the part of students, the claim that Esperanto is especially appropriate for students with special needs, that the study of Esperanto will encourage students to study other languages, and that Esperanto may be able to be taught more efficiently and explicitly than could be national/ethnic languages. It is important to note that the lack of empirical evidence with regard to these claims in no way suggests that they are untrue; rather, we are left in these cases with (sometimes quite compelling) anecdotal evidence and personal experience in evaluating them. Further, while the research base with respect to the teaching and learning of Esperanto suffers from some serious shortcomings, the same could be argued with respect to the teaching and learning of virtually all other languages, especially in the cases of the less commonly taught languages.

CONCLUDING COMMENTS

Esperanto, as was noted at the beginning of this chapter, is indeed a fascinating phenomenon. On one hand, it is clear that it has not lived up to Zamenhof's hopes as a widely used, international auxiliary language. At the same time, one might argue that while *as a language,* Esperanto functions quite effectively, *as a movement* it has not yet proven its case. Further, there are a large number of cases in the twentieth century that provide ample evidence that while language can sometimes be a barrier to communication, and can create problems of understanding between groups, all too often the problems and tensions between groups are largely extralinguistic in nature—as the case of the breakup of Yugoslavia, where the different ethnic groups arguably speak different varieties of what could be—and in fact, was—considered a common language, makes only too clear (see Lampe, 2000). To be fair, though, Zamenhof did not believe that language was the only problem in relations among groups; merely an important one, and in that he was certainly correct. Of perhaps greater concern for language educators is the potential value of Esperanto as a means of facilitating language study—not only in terms of its propaedeutic effects, but also as a way of introducing students to language and language study in a context in which success is fairly easily and rapid, at least when compared with the study of other languages (see D. Richardson, 1988, pp. 21-22). Finally, Esperanto provides language educators with an important case study of language, language attitudes, and the symbolic value of language (see Nuessel, 1996).

NOTES

1. The preparation of this chapter was made possible in part by a grant from the Esperantic Studies Foundation. I am particularly grateful for the comments and suggestions offered by Alvino E. Fantini, Frank Nuessel, Humphrey Tonkin, and Jonathan Pool.
2. Klingon is a supposedly alien (i.e., nonhuman) language created for the *Star Trek* television series. There is currently a dictionary and grammar for Klingon (see Okrand, 1992), as well as a Klingon Language Insitute, a correspondence course for learning Klingon, a summer language camp, and numerous translation projects.
3. I am grateful to Pádraig Ó Riagáin, of the Institiúid Teangeolaiochta Éireann (The Linguistics Institute of Ireland), for pointing out, in the case of Irish, the valuable distinction between a *speech community* and a *speech network*.
4. There is an ambiguity in English possible here. The meaning of the term here is *to be being drunk*, as in *La akvo trinkiĝas,* The water is being drunk or *La akvo trinkiĝis,* The water was being drunk. Thus, *trinkiĝadi* means to keep being drunk (i.e., consumed by drinking). This has nothing whatsoever to do with *drunk* as in *inebriated*, which would be expressed in Esperanto using the word *ebria*.
5. It should be noted that some pedagogical texts present the two tables as a single "Table of Correlatives" (see, e.g., Cresswell & Hartley, 1992, pp. 188-189; Nuessel, 2000, p. 51; D. Richardson, 1988, p. 127).

APPENDIX A: THE SIXTEEN RULES OF ESPERANTO

The "Sixteen Rules" are found in a wide variety of sources. The version provided here is based on Zamenhof's (1905/1963) *Fundamento de Esperanto.*

1. There is no indefinite, and only one definite, article, *la*, for all genders, numbers, and cases.
2. Nouns are formed by adding *-o* to the root. For the plural, *-j* must be added to the singular. There are two cases: the nominative and the objective (accusative). The root with the added *-o* is the nominative, the objective adds an *-n* after the *-o*. Other cases are formed by prepositions.
3. Adjectives are formed by adding *-a* to the root. The numbers and cases are the same as in nouns. The comparative degree is formed by prefixing *pli* "more"; the superlative by *plej* "most." "Than" is rendered by *ol*.
4. The cardinal numerals do not change their forms for the different cases. They are: *unu, du, tri, kvar, kvin, ses, sep, ok, naŭ, dek, cent, mil.* The tens and hundreds are formed by simple junction of the numerals. Ordinals are formed by adding the adjectival *-a* to the cardinals. Multiplicatives add the suffix *-obl-;* fractionals add the suffix *-on-;* collective numerals add *-op-;* for distributives the word *po* is used. The numerals can also be used as nouns or adverbs with the appropriate endings.
5. The personal pronouns are: *mi, vi, li, ŝi, ĝi* (for inanimate objects and animals), *si* (reflexive), *ni, vi, ili, oni* (indefinite). Possessive pronouns are formed by suffixing the adjectival termination. The declension of pronouns is identical with that of nouns.
6. The verb does not change its form for numbers or persons. The present tense ends in *-as,* the past in *-is,* the future in *-os,* the conditional in *-us,* the imperative in *-u,* the infinitive in *-i.* Active participles, both adjectival and adverbial, are formed by adding, in the present, *-ant-*, in the past *-int-*, and in the future *-ont-*. The passive forms are, respectively, *-at-, -it-, and -ot-*. All forms of the passive are rendered by the respective forms of the verb *esti* (to be) and the passive participle of the required verb. The preposition used is *de.*
7. Adverbs are formed by adding *-e* to the root. The degrees of comparison are the same as in adjectives.
8. All prepositions take the nominative case.
9. Every word is to be read exactly as written.
10. The accent falls on the penultimate syllable.
11. Compound words are formed by simple junction of roots (the principal word standing last). Grammatical terminations are regarded as independent words.
12. If there is one negative in a clause, a second is not admissible.

13. To show direction, words take the termination of the objective case.
14. Every preposition has a definite fixed meaning; but if it is necessary to use a preposition, and it is not quite evident from the sense which it should be, the word *je* is used, which has no definite meaning. Instead of *je*, the objective without a preposition may be used.
15. The so-called foreign words (words that the greater number of languages have derived from the same source) undergo no change in the international language, beyond conforming to its system of orthography.
16. The final vowel of the noun and the article may be dropped and replaced with an apostrophe.

APPENDIX B: THE ESPERANTO ALPHABET

The Esperanto alphabet consists of 28 letters:

a	[a]
b	[b ɔ]
c	[ts ɔ]
ĉ	[tʃɔ]
d	[d ɔ]
e	[ɛ]
f	[f ɔ]
g	[g ɔ]
ĝ	[dʒɔ]
h	[h ɔ]
ĥ	[x ɔ]
i	[i]
j	[j ɔ]
ĵ	[ʒɔ]
k	[k ɔ]
l	[l ɔ]
m	[m ɔ]
n	[n ɔ]
o	[ɔ]
p	[p ɔ]
r	[r ɔ]
s	[s ɔ]
ŝ	[ʃɔ]

t	[t ɔ]
u	[u]
ŭ	[w ɔ]
v	[v ɔ]
z	[z ɔ]

CHAPTER 7

WHERE HAVE ALL THE LANGUAGES GONE?

Language Endangerment and Language Death[1]

During the coming century, according to some informed estimates, 3,000 of the existing 6,000 languages will perish and another 2,400 will come near to extinction. This leaves just 600 languages in the "safe" category, assuming that category to be languages having 100,000 speakers or more. Thus, 90 percent of the world's languages are imperiled.... Languages in this situation are typically "local" languages, as opposed to national or international languages, and in the minds of many people, both linguists and non-linguists, their endangerment and progressive extinction amount to a catastrophe for human intellectual and cultural diversity, a disaster comparable in its extent to losses in other aspects of our environment.

—*Ken Hale* (1998, p. 192)

Beginning with the publication of Michael Krauss' article, "The World's Languages in Crisis," published in the influential linguistics journal *Language* in 1992, the related issues of language endangerment and language death have become increasingly popular topics among linguists and other writers with an interest in language matters. These topics were, of course,

Critical Questions, Critical Perspectives:
Language and the Second Language Educator, 103–118

not new; linguists had been conducting serious research on language endangerment for a considerable period. What has changed has been the extent to which the audience for such works has become a popular one. Indeed, in the past decade, a number of books have appeared on these matters, often with quite apocalyptic-sounding titles: Mark Abley's (2003) *Spoken Here: Travels among Threatened Languages,* David Crystal's (2000) *Language Death,* Andrew Dalby's (2003) *Language in Danger: The Loss of Linguistic Diversity and the Threat to Our Future,* R. M. W. Dixon's (1997) *The rise and fall of languages,* Lenore Grenoble and Lindsay Whaley's (1998a) edited volume *Endangered Languages,* Claude Hagège's (2000) *Halte à la mort des langues,* Anita Hertzfeld and Yolanda Lastra's (1999) edited book *Las causas sociales de la desaparición y del mantenimento de las lenguas en las naciones de América,* Mark Janse and Sijmen Tol's edited book (2003) *Language Death and Language Maintenance,* Daniel Nettle and Suzanne Romaine's (2000) *Vanishing Voices: The Extinction of the World's Languages,* and Tove Skutnabb-Kangas' (2000) *Linguistic genocide in education,* among others. To be sure, the issue of language endangerment is a real one, and it is one with profound implications. If the commonly cited estimates are to be believed, more than half of the approximately 6,000 languages in the world today are likely to disappear in the present century, and on at least one pessimistic account, as few as 600 languages may survive in the long term (see Krauss, 1992).

The fact of language endangerment is all too real, although our ability to predict the fate of individual languages remains problematic at best. As William Mackey has recently reminded us,

> the trouble with most appropriated models of language change is that they fail to reflect the multidimensional and multifunctional nature of language dynamics ... language as behaviour is a multidimensional and multifunctional system of mutually modifying practices. If we could quantify these practices and plot the results on a time scale, we could perhaps extrapolate the curve with a tolerable margin of error over the short term. But whatever is projected would still be subject to changes in its own environment, which by the nature of things could be triggered by the unpredictable behaviour of people and compounded by the hazards of history. (2003, pp. 78-79)

If our predictions and forecasts are inevitably uncertain, though, this does not mean that we do not have a good overall picture of what is happening worldwide to language diversity, and that picture is not an encouraging one. There are a number of different ways in which threatened languages can be categorized. The most common, and widely accepted, categorization is that of Krauss (1992), who distinguished among safe languages, endangered languages, moribund languages, and extinct languages (see Crystal, 2000, pp. 20-21; for an alternative model, see

Grenoble & Whaley, 1998b). The safe languages are those which have sufficient population bases to ensure their long-term survival—languages like English, French, Russian, Spanish, and so on. In some instances, relatively small languages (that is, small in terms of numbers of speakers) are also safe languages because of their status as official languages, their role as a marker of ethnic or national identity, their use in government, business and educational spheres, and so on. Thus, although Danish is spoken by a fairly small population, it is not, at least in the short and medium-term, endangered. Of course, such languages are nonetheless potentially at risk, as Johan Van Hoorde of the Nederlandse Taalunie points out with respect to Dutch:

> Dutch may not be threatened with extinction in the short or medium term, but it is in danger of losing domains. It could eventually become just a colloquial language, a language you use at home to speak with your family—the language you can best express your emotions in—but not the one you use for the serious things in life: money, science, technology. (1998, p. 6)

ENDANGERED LANGUAGES

Endangered languages are those languages which are faced with a more immediate threat to their survival. Although size alone does not adequately indicate the extent to which a particular language is threatened or endangered, it is a relatively strong indicator in most instances (see Nettle & Romaine, 2000, pp. 8-10; see also Nettle, 1999, p. 114). Consider the estimates in Table 7.1, which are based on data in *Ethnologue* (see Crystal, 2000, p. 15):

Table 7.1

Number of Native Speakers	*Number of Languages*
Languages with more than 100 million speakers	8
Languages with 10 million to 99.9 million speakers	72
Languages with 1 million to 9.9 million speakers	239
Languages with 100,000 to 999,999 speakers	795
Languages with 10,000 to 99,999 speakers	1,605
Languages with 1,000 to 9,999 speakers	1,782
Languages with 100 to 999 speakers	1,075
Languages with 10 to 99 speakers	302
Languages with 1 to 9 speakers	181

The eight languages with more than 100 million native speakers are, perhaps not surprisingly, Mandarin Chinese, Spanish, English, Portuguese, Russian, Japanese, Bengali, and Hindi—which together account for some 2.4 billion individuals. These languages are of course safe, as in fact are those in the next two or three categories. Languages with fewer than 20,000 native speakers are considered potentially endangered, which means that two thirds of the languages currently spoken in the world fall into this category. In fact, this may, in the medium to long term, be a conservative estimate; languages with 100,000 speakers or fewer can hardly be described in most instances as thriving, let alone safe. Another way to think about this, and one which emphasizes the significance of the problem, is that 96% of the world's languages are spoken by 4% of the human population (Crystal, 2000, p. 14).

MORIBUND LANGUAGES

The key difference between an endangered language and a moribund language is that the latter type of language is no longer being learned as a native language by children. In his landmark article, Krauss (1992) illustrates the challenge of moribund languages by reference to the indigenous languages of North America: the are a total of 187 indigenous languages in North America, all of which would currently be considered at least endangered. Of these 187 languages, though, only 38 are being passed on to the next generation. In other words, more than 80% of the indigenous languages on our continent are already moribund—that is, they are on a fast track to extinction.

LANGUAGE EXTINCTION

Languages become extinct, in a nutshell, when they no longer have speakers. To some extent, one could argue that since language is inherently social, a language dies not when the last native speaker dies, but rather, when the next-to-last native speaker dies. As David Crystal has commented, "as speakers cannot demonstrate their fluency if they have no one to talk to, a language is effectively dead when there is only one speaker left" (2000, p. 11). In any event, languages can and do die, and are doing so at a fairly rapid rate. Krauss, after a very careful statistical analysis, concludes that, "I consider it a plausible calculation that—at the rate things are going—the coming century will see either the death or the doom of 90% of mankind's languages" (1992, p. 7).

REFLECTIONS ON LANGUAGE ENDANGERMENT AND LANGUAGE DEATH

Why, though, should language endangerment and language death be of any particular interest for or concern to second/foreign language educators? After all, the languages most commonly taught—and indeed, even most of those that are less commonly taught, as we saw earlier in Chapter 5—are in no real danger. Spanish, French, even German and Russian, will continue to thrive for the foreseeable future, even if in some instances the popularity of German and Russian, and even of French, as second/foreign languages in the U.S. context is not what it once was.

The answer has to do not so much with the particular features of any particular language, but rather, with those of language in general. More to the point, if different languages in essence construct reality in somewhat different ways, offering distinct epistemological lenses for understanding the world, then there is considerable value in knowing as much as we can about the range of possible ways in which human beings, through human language, can indeed construct our realities. As Vjaceslav Ivanov has commented,

> Each language constitutes a certain model of the universe, a semiotic system of understanding the world, and if we have 4,000 different ways to describe the world, this makes us rich. We should be concerned about preserving languages just as we are about ecology. (quoted in Crystal, 2000, p. 36)

The commonly used analogy between language health and language death and the health and status of biological species, which is widely employed in discussions about language endangerment, is a powerful one, though not one without problems. However, in both instances it is understandable that many people do not see a problem with allowing extinction, which is, of course, in its own way, a *natural* process. However, a number of linguists have offered powerful and compelling arguments in recent years for why language diversity is important and worth preserving (see Abley, 2003; Crystal, 2000; Dalby, 2003; Dixon, 1997; Grenoble & Whaley, 1998a; Hagège, 2000; Janse & Tol, 2003; Nettle & Romaine, 2000; Skutnabb-Kangas, 2000). Apart from the obvious value of linguistic diversity for the study and understanding of human language in general, there are a number of other reasons for being concerned with the loss of linguistic diversity in our world:

- Languages express identity in a unique and important way. Although ethnicity is not inevitably tied to language, language difference nevertheless does play an important role in the maintenance of ethnic identity.

- Languages are, in the words of David Crystal, "repositories of history." The history of a people is embedded and reflected in its language.
- Languages also contain unique knowledge about the natural, physical world around us. Since many of the languages which are endangered are found in areas of the world where there is extensive biological diversity, often unexplored, the languages themselves provide potentially irreplaceable information about the natural world.

Linguists, it should be noted, generally see themselves on the side of the angels with respect to language endangerment and language death. And yet, the reality is a bit more complex than this might suggest. In a very powerful article titled, "The Endangered Languages Issue as a Hopeless Cause," Paul Newman argues that linguists are, as a professional community, doing very little to address this challenge. He cites the comic strip character Pogo, who once observed that "we has seen the enemy, and it is us." Newman suggests that in the case of endangered languages linguists are actually responsible for making the situation worse rather than ameliorating it. His argument focuses in part of the culture of linguistics as a discipline, and in particular on the relatively low emphasis on fieldwork in the profession, as part of the problem. His conclusion is bleak:

> Despite the best intentions of many well-meaning and dedicated linguists, the rapid disappearance of languages throughout the world is likely to continue unabated ... [we] are up against a formidable enemy—and that enemy is our own discipline of linguistics and the individuals who make it up. We can continue to talk about the matter, as surely will be done *ad nauseum* at one international meeting or workshop after another; but given the odds against us, the chances of concrete results are pitifully small. (2003, p. 11).

THE PARADOXICAL CASE OF AMERICAN SIGN LANGUAGE

I want to explore a rather unusual—and, in fact, only potential rather than real or current—case of language endangerment at this point. American Sign Language (ASL) is the vernacular language of the U.S. Deaf[2] community, which is by far among the most organized and successful in the world, but it is by no means unique in either its fundamental nature or in its objectives. Comparable Deaf cultural communities exist throughout the world, distinguished both from one another by their respective languages and cultural contexts and from the surrounding hearing communities with which they interact (see Fischer & Lane, 1993; Kyle & Woll, 1985). Both in the United States and elsewhere, an extensive, and rapidly growing, literature has not only documented but begun analyzing each of the many elements of the Deaf cultural community. Central to such efforts have been the study and analysis of natural sign languages. Although the growth in our knowledge about the cultures and languages of the Deaf is certainly both impressive and valuable, it is perhaps less significant than the themes which underlie it. Central to these themes has been the concern with the role of language in domination and power relations as these relate to deaf-hearing interaction (see S. Ball, 1990; Foucault, 1972). As Harlan Lane, speaking not only for himself but for many scholars concerned with the Deaf as a cultural and linguistic community, has argued:

> I maintain that the vocabulary and conceptual framework our society has customarily used with regard to deaf people, based as it is on infirmity, serves us and the members of the deaf community less well than a vocabulary and framework of cultural relativity. I want to replace the normativeness of medicine with the curiosity of ethnography. (1992, p. 19)

Also of significance in understanding a sociocultural model of deafness is the rejection by advocates of this view of the paternalism that has tended to characterize discussions which take place within the more common pathological model of deafness. As Harlan Hahn has compellingly argued with respect to paternalism toward disabled people in general,

> Paternalism enables the dominant elements of a society to express profound and sincere sympathy for the members of a minority group while, at the same time, keeping them in a position of social and economic subordination. It has allowed the nondisabled to act as the protectors, guides, leaders, role-models, and intermediaries for disabled individuals who, like children, are often assumed to be helpless, dependent, asexual, economically unproductive, physically limited, emotionally immature, and acceptable only when they are unobtrusive.... Politically, disabled people usually have been neither seen nor heard. Paternalistic attitudes, therefore, may be primarily responsible both for the ironic invisibility of disabled persons and for the prior tendency to ignore this important area of public policy. (1986, p. 130)

Applying this concern with paternalism to the specific case of the Deaf, we find that:

> Like the paternalism of the colonizers, hearing paternalism begins with defective perception, because it superimposes its image of the familiar world of hearing people on the unfamiliar world of deaf people. Hearing paternalism likewise sees its task as "civilizing" its charges: restoring deaf people to society. And hearing paternalism fails to understand the structure and values of deaf society. The hearing people who control the affairs of deaf children and adults commonly do not know deaf people and do not want to. Since they cannot see deaf people as they really are, they make up imaginary deaf people of their own, in accord with their own experiences and needs. Paternalism deals in such stereotypes. (Lane, 1992, p. 37)

Since the 1960 publication of Stokoe's landmark study, *Sign Language Structures* (see Stokoe, 1993), there has been a veritable explosion of linguistic, psycholinguistic, and sociolinguistic research dealing with ASL, as well as with other natural sign languages. The result is that we know far more about the nature and workings of natural sign languages than we did 40-odd years ago. As Liddell notes in his recent book on grammar, gesture, and meaning in ASL:

> By the early 1970s many other linguists and psychologists began studying the properties of ASL. At that time, their published papers tended to begin with brief justifications explaining that ASL was a language. Such explanations were needed since most people still held the view that ASL was not a language. By perhaps the mid-seventies, and most certainly by the early eighties, the weight of published descriptions of ASL and its grammar was sufficient to turn the tide of opinion about the language status of ASL. Studies of various aspects of the grammar of ASL left no doubt that signers using ASL were using a real human language.... The recognition that sign languages were real human languages set off a flurry of activity in a number of academic arenas beginning in the seventies.... More and more sign languages continue to be identified and investigated as researchers around the globe pursue answers to a wide variety of interesting scientific questions. (Liddell, 2003, pp. 4-5)

It is obviously not possible to provide anything like a comprehensive overview of what linguists have discovered about ASL and other natural sign languages. However, it is both possible and useful, I believe, to present a brief discussion of some of the principal, and generally common, linguistic features of natural sign languages. Because the greatest amount of linguistic research to date has been concerned with ASL, this discussion will necessarily focus on ASL, although examples from other sign languages will be provided as appropriate. The five broad topics to be examined here are signs as lexical items, spatial relations in sign language syntax, the role and use of classifiers in sign languages, the diversity of sign languages, and threats to ASL.

Signs as Lexical Items

Signs constitute the lexicon of sign language; they are, as it were, the *words* of sign language. One of the basic principals of all human languages is, "that the symbols that make up the language can be broken down into smaller parts" (Valli & Lucas, 2000, p. 19; see also Battison, 1978). The study of the smallest contrastive units of language is phonology. In English, for instance, a word like *cats* consists of four phonemes: /k/, /a/, /t/, and /s/. For a spoken language, a phoneme is the smallest contrastive unit of sound; in sign languages, the phonemes are based on the five fundamental components, or parameters, of the sign. These five fundamental parameters include handshape, movement, palm orientation, location, and nonmanual features. A change in any one of these parameters can constitute a change in the meaning of the sign, just as the change of a single phoneme can change the meaning of a word in a spoken language. Cat, cot, and kit, for instance, differ only in a single phoneme in English. In ASL, the signs SUMMER[3] and DRY are distinguished only by location, RED and CUTE are distinguished only by handshape, SHORT and TRAIN are distinguished only by palm orientation, and SIT and CHAIR are distinguished only by movement.

Although it would seem to be obvious, it is important to explain here explicitly that signs are generally concept based in nature. In other words, just as there is no exact parallel in meaning between words in Spanish and English, so there will be no exact parallel between a spoken language and a sign language. In the case of ASL, there are instances in which ASL is more precise than English, and other instances in which English is more precise than ASL. For example, the English word *run* is translated in ASL by a number of semantically different and distinct signs:

I'm going to *run* in the Boston Marathon next year.

Is it true that Harry is planning to *run* for the vacant Senate seat?

Mary Anne has always *run* her business efficiently.

My wife has a *run* in her stocking.

This apartment doesn't even have *running* water.

My nose is *runny*.

At the same time, the basic ASL sign CONTROL can, depending on the context in which it is used, mean not only control, but also direct, manage, administer, administrate, govern, or regulate. This lack of one-to-one correspondence in the lexicons of different languages is neither unusual nor surprising; the student of French quickly learns that she *has hunger* in French (*avoir faim*) even though she *is hungry* in English. The point at which this does become problematic is with the manual sign codes. Since such systems are deliberately constructed to mimic the spoken language, they generally adhere to a one word to one sign correspondence. Although this may facilitate the learning of the manual sign code by hearing people, it creates a certain potential for confusion for those who already sign in a natural sign language.

Spatial Relations in Sign Language Syntax

Because sign language takes place visually and gesturally, physical space can and does play an incredibly important role not only in terms of the parameters of particular signs (movement, location, and palm orientation are all, ultimately, possible because of the use of physical space in sign language), but also in the syntax of sign language (see Emmorey & Reilly, 1995a; Liddell, 2003; Neidle, Kegl, Maclaughlin, Bahan, & Lee, 2000). As Emmorey and Reilly have argued, "space is a unique resource available to the visual-manual modality" (1995b, p. 2). Liddell has gone even further, pointing out that

> Considerable effort has been devoted to exploring the striking parallels between the structure of spoken languages and sign languages on virtually every level. There is, however, one aspect of ASL for which there exists no obvious parallel in any spoken language. ASL, and apparently all other natural sign languages, allow signers to produce signs at, or direct signs toward, different locations within the signing space to indicate specific referents or to show specific locations. Pronouns, indicating verbs, locative verbs, and classifier predicates, all have this capability. Producing such signs at or directing such signs toward specific parts of the signing space produces meanings that differ from those of the same signs produced at or directed toward other areas of the signing space. (Liddell, 1995, p. 19)

Perhaps the most fundamental use of space in sign language, beyond its use in the composition of particular signs, is the identification of *signing space* itself. Signing space refers to the area roughly from the signer's waist to about six inches over the head, and from the lax arm spread of the signer on both sides. It is within this space that signing occurs; moving one's hands out of the signing space is an indication that one is finished signing and is ready to be addressed. There is also a secondary signing space in which fingerspelling normally takes place.

One of the ways in which time is indicated in sign language is through the use of the *time line*, which allows for the expression of relative time. Thus, in ASL, there is an imaginary line running through the body of the signer and continuing both in front of and behind the signer. Events are *placed* along this time line, which ranges from the distant past (as in *once upon a time*) through the present and on to the far future. Specific time signs (NOW, TODAY, TOMORROW, YESTERDAY, LAST-WEEK, NEXT-MONTH, etc.) will fall along this time line. In the case of British Sign Language, it has been suggested that there may in fact be four time lines functioning in slightly different ways. The first time line is essentially comparable to the ASL time line. The second runs from the signer's elbow to fingertips on the nondominant arm, and is used to express BEFORE, AFTER, and WEEK. The third time line runs in front of the signer from left to right, and is used to indicate continuity (e.g., FOREVER) and duration (e.g., CONTINUOUS). Finally, the fourth time line, which is located from head to foot on the signer's dominant side, is used only to describe human growing or maturation (e.g., CHILD, ADULT) (see Sutton-Spence & Woll, 1998, pp. 183-185). In both ASL and British Sign Language, the past is behind the signer and the future is in front of the signer, but there are other natural sign languages in which this is reversed, presumably because we already know (and so can, in a sense, see) the past, but the future is unknown to us (and hence unseen).

Their spatial organization makes it easy for sign languages to develop relatively complex pronominal systems. Liddell (2003, pp. 20-34), for instance, has identified a total of 26 pronominal signs in ASL, and the real number is almost certainly higher. ASL pronouns fall into two distinct person categories: first person and nonfirst person.[4] Within these broad categories, there are singular, dual, multiple (3, 4, and 5), and generic plural pronouns, as well as possessive and emphatic pronouns. There are also reflexive pronouns. Thus, ASL allows for considerable precision with respect to different pronominal signs. There are, for example, distinct signs for THE-TWO-OF-US, THE-THREE-OF-US, THE-FOUR-OF-US, THE-FIVE-OF-US as well as a generic first person plural pronoun. The spatial organization of sign language facilitates this, and also explains why there is no need for a syntactic distinction between the second and third person pronouns. In addition, spatial organization allows for the placement of signs (including pronouns) on a 180° arc in front of the signer. This referential framework (which can be either fixed or shifting in nature) allows for the placement of multiple individuals or places, and thus serves as a valuable component for narrative discourse. This referential framework is also interesting in that two signers can share the same referential framework in a given conversation (see Neidle et al., 2000, pp. 30-32).

The spatial organization of sign languages also allows certain verbs to indicate directionality; thus, I-ASK-YOU and YOU-ASK-ME are distinguished in ASL only by the direction of movement of the sign (the former moves out from the signer toward the other person, while the latter moves from the other person to the signer). Other directional verbs in ASL include ANSWER, GIVE, LOOK-AT, BOTHER, CRITICIZE, TEACH, and so on. Finally, the spatial organization of sign language also allows for directional verbs to indicate reciprocity, as in THEY-LOOK-AT-EACH-OTHER or WE-INFORM-EACH-OTHER.

Classifiers in Sign Languages

Classifiers are not unique to sign languages, and in fact they play important roles in a number of well-studied spoken languages, including Mandarin Chinese (Po-Ching & Rimmington, 1997, pp. 15-19), Cantonese (Matthews & Yip, 1994, pp. 92-107), and Thai (Smyth, 2002, pp. 31-38), among others. They are extraordinarily important in sign languages as well, and operate a bit differently than those found in spoken languages (see Emmorey, 2003). In essence, in the context of the study of sign languages, a classifier is a generic handshape that is used, generally pronominally, for a class of related objects. Thus, as Schein and Stewart explain,

> Classifiers are ASL signs that represent specific locations and/or movements of a person or a thing. The signer uses the classifier to indicate the action of the person or thing being described. For example, a teenage describing how his car hit a tree would first sign or spell CAR and thereafter would use the classifier handshape VEHICLE to show the movement of the car leading up to the accident. The classifer VEHICLE can be used to mean "car", "bus", "truck", "boat", or any type of conveyance. It can be moved in any direction to indicate the action of the vehicle being discussed. Classifiers also represent the size, shape, and other characteristics of a person or thing. (Schein & Stewart, 1995, pp. 49-50)

ASL has a large variety of classifiers for such concepts as a (generic) person, a person with legs, a vehicle, an airplane, a stationary object, a flat object that doesn't move, a flat object that can move or be moved, a cup or glass, and so on. Among their other uses, classifiers are especially useful as new terminology needs to be developed.

The Diversity of Sign Languages

The diversity of sign languages actually refers to a number of different, and significant, kinds of diversity. First, there are large numbers of sign languages that are natural sign languages used by deaf people in different settings around the world. Although these different natural sign languages share certain generic features (such as their gestural and visual nature, their use of space for linguistic purposes, etc.), and while some sign languages are genetically related to others (that is, there are sign language families just as there are spoken language families),[5] these languages are nevertheless distinctive languages in their own right. Many of these natural sign languages have been studied by linguists; among these are not only ASL, but also Australian Sign Language, British Sign Language, Danish Sign Language, Dutch Sign Language, French Sign Language, German Sign Language, Hausa Sign Language, Hong Kong Sign Language, Indo-Pakistani Sign Language, Israeli Sign Language, Italian Sign Language, Kenyan Sign Language, Russian Sign Language, South African Sign Language, Swedish Sign Language, Taiwanese Sign Language, Thai Sign Language, and Venezuelan Sign Language, and this is far from an exhaustive list. Indeed, although impressive in its own right, this list is but the proverbial tip of the iceberg, since most natural sign languages (like most spoken languages) remain unstudied. Skutnabb-Kangas has reminded us that, "there probably are something between 6,500 and 10,000 spoken (oral) languages in the world, and a number of sign languages which can be equally large" (2000, p. 30).

The numbers of natural sign languages are but one sense in which we can talk about sign language diversity, however. The second way in which diversity enters the picture is with respect to the diversity present *within* particular natural sign languages. In the case of ASL, for instance, we know that there is not only extensive lexical diversity related to region of the country, but also diversity related to age, gender, and ethnicity (see Lucas, Bayley, & Valli, 2001). A far more extreme case is provided by South African Sign Language (SASL). SASL, at least in part as a consequence of the social and educational policies of the apartheid regime, is characterized by extensive lexical variation coupled with an underlying syntactic unity. As Penn and Reagan have noted,

> Of the 2500 lexical items collected under the auspices of the SASLRP [South African Sign Language Research Programme] for the dictionary of SASL, only 2% of all of the words represented had a single, common sign across all the different deaf groups, and roughly 10% of the words have as few as one or two signed variants ... On average, six variants per word were found and the range went as high as eleven variants [for a single word]. (Penn & Reagan, 2001, p. 55)

Indeed, the situation is so complex that sign language linguists concerned with SASL actually engaged in arguments about whether it is a single sign language, or whether it is a related collection of different sign languages (see Aarons & Akach, 2002; Branson & Miller, 2002, pp. 244-245).

The third sort of diversity that plays a role in understanding sign language is not so much a diversity in terms of sign language as it is a diversity with respect to *signing*. The distinction between sign language and signing is in fact a very significant one. Up to this point, we have been concerned only with natural sign languages—the sign languages that emerge and are used in communities of deaf people for intragroup communication. The deaf, however, do not live apart from the hearing: rather, they are integrated into the hearing world in a number of ways and on a number of different levels. The vast majority of deaf people have hearing parents, and the vast majority of deaf people will have hearing children. In addition, the deaf need to have access to at least some other hearing people in order to function socially and economically. While the children of deaf people may well learn their parents' sign language as a native language, most parents of deaf children and other hearing people who are in contact with the deaf will generally not learn the natural sign language. Instead, they will learn to sign using what is in essence a contact sign language—that is, a sign language that has elements of both the natural sign language and the surrounding spoken language (see Lucas & Valli, 1989, 1991, 1992). Such contact languages, originally labeled *pidgin sign*, are in fact the primary kind of sign language used in hearing-deaf communicative interchanges. These contact languages, like natural sign languages, are the result of normal linguistic development, and their emergence parallels that of spoken contact languages. Finally, there have been efforts to design "manual sign codes" to represent spoken languages (see Bornstein, 1990; Reagan, 1995a). These manual sign codes are simply efforts to represent a spoken language in a gestural/visual modality—comparable, really, to writing a spoken language. Manual sign codes were developed in educational settings as a way of providing deaf children with access to spoken language. In the U.S. case, for instance, the most popular of these manual sign codes is Signing Exact English (SEE-II) (Gustason & Zawolkow, 1993); in Britain, the Paget-Gorman system essentially served the same purpose, albeit on a somewhat less sophisticated level (see Paget, 1951). It is important to note that manual sign codes are just that: codes to represent language, not language in and of themselves (see Reagan, 1995a, 2001b). The actual educational value of such manual sign codes is actually somewhat debatable, but to a fluent signer, the codes are often perceived as slow, awkward and confusing.

Threats to ASL

This brings us back to the issue of whether ASL is indeed an endangered language. At the present time, ASL's status would appear to be fairly secure. More than half a million individuals, by some accounts, are users of ASL, and the language is clearly being passed on both intergenerationally and intragenerationally (one of the ways in which ASL, and other natural sign languages, are unique has to do with such atypical patterns of transmission). ASL is also growing in popularity as a curricular offering in both secondary schools and colleges and universities, and its public visibility has arguably never been higher. And yet, the language is nevertheless potentially at risk. It is at risk as efforts to medicalize deafness continue, and as hearing professionals continue to seek to find *cures* for deafness—cochlear implants being just one of the possible options now available. ASL, in short, is at risk precisely because its users are seen not as a linguistic minority, but rather as *disabled*.

CONCLUSION

In this chapter, we have explored some of the more important aspects of language endangerment and language death. Our examination of the special case of ASL makes clear that the challenges of language endangerment may be closer to home than many might suspect, but also makes clear the important role of identity and constructions of identity for language maintenance. Such issues, as the others addressed earlier in this book, are in fact of central concern for all of us, not only as language educators but as citizens in an increasingly complex global world.

NOTES

1. The title of this chapter was also used in Nettle and Romaine (2000).
2. In this chapter, I have followed the common practice of distinguishing between audiological *deafness*, which is represented with a lowercase "d," and cultural *Deafness*, which is represented with an uppercase "D." Although this is not the place for the case to be argued, the question of whether the Deaf community constitutes a *culture* in an anthropological sense is, in my view, beyond question. The Deaf cultural community is demonstrably characterized by the same kinds of elements that characterize any other cultural community, including a common, shared language (ASL), a shared awareness of Deaf cultural identity, distinctive behavioral norms and patterns, cultural artifacts, endogamous marital patterns, a shared historical knowledge and awareness, and a network of voluntary, in-group social organizations (see R. Baker & Battison, 1980; Lane, 1992; Lucas, 1989; Neisser, 1983; Padden & Humphries, 1988; Reagan, 1985, 1990, 1992a; Sacks, 1989; Schein, 1989; Stokoe, 1980; Woodward, 1982).
3. I have followed the common practice of indicating a particular sign by writing its English meaning in capital letters (e.g., BOY). It should be noted that many signs require multiple English words to represent a single sign; in these instances, the English words are joined by hyphens to indi-

cate that although there are several English words used to express the meaning of the sign, there is only a single sign (e.g., I-ASK-YOU).

4. The idea that ASL employs a two, rather than three, person pronoun system is relatively recent. Much of the early work on the structure of ASL suggested that ASL, like English, had a three-person pronoun system. More recent work, however, has provided compelling evidence to the contrary. See Meier (1990) and Liddell (2003, pp. 20-26) in particular.
5. See Woll, Sutton-Spence and Elton (2001), for a discussion of the historical relationships among sign languages.

REFERENCES

Aarons, D., & Akach, P. (2002). South African Sign Language: One language or many? In R. Mesthrie (Ed.), *Language in South Africa* (pp. 127-147). Cambridge, England: Cambridge University Press.

Abley, M. (2003). *Spoken here: Travels among threatened languages.* Boston: Houghton Mifflin.

Achard, P. (1993). *La sociologie du langage* [The sociology of language]. Paris: Presses Universitaires de France.

Ager, D., Muskens, G., & Wright, S. (Eds.). (1993). *Language education for intercultural communication.* Clevedon, England: Multilingual Matters.

Allen, R. (1992). Teaching Arabic in the United States: Past, present, and future. In A. Rouchdy (Ed.), *The Arabic language in America* (pp. 222-250). Detroit, MI: Wayne State University Press.

Allen, W. (1980). *Side effects.* New York: Ballentine.

Almond, B. (1993). Rights. In P. Singer (Ed.), *A companion to ethics* (pp. 259-269). Oxford, England: Basil Blackwell.

Altmann, G. (1997). *The ascent of Babel: An exploration of language, mind, and understanding.* Oxford, England: Oxford University Press.

Ammon, U. (2003). Global English and the non-native speaker: Overcoming disadvantage. In H. Tonkin & T. Reagan (Eds.), *Language in the 21st Century* (pp. 23-34). Amsterdam: John Benjamins.

Andrews, L. (1998). *Language exploration and awareness: A resource book for teachers* (2nd ed.). Mahwah, NJ: Erlbaum.

Appel, R., & Muysken, P. (1987). *Language contact and bilingualism.* London: Edward Arnold.

Apple, M., & Beane, J. (Eds.). (1995). *Democratic schools.* Alexandria, VA: Association for Supervision and Curriculum Development.

Arndt, W. (1972). *Pushkin threefold: Narrative, lyric, polemic and ribald verse.* Dana Point, CA: Ardis.

Audi, R. (Ed.). (1995). *The Cambridge dictionary of philosophy.* Cambridge, England: Cambridge University Press.

Audi, R. (1998). *Epistemology: A contemporary introduction to the theory of knowledge.* London: Routledge.

Auld, W. (1988). *La fenomeno esperanto* [The Esperanto phenomenon]. Rotterdam: Universala Esperanto-Asocio.

Baker, Charlotte, & Cokely, D. (1980). *American Sign Language: A teacher's resource text on grammar and culture.* Silver Spring, MD: T. J.

Baker, Colin. (2001). *Foundations of bilingual education and bilingualism* (3rd ed.). Clevedon, England: Multilingual Matters.

Baker, C., & Battison, R. (Eds.). (1980). *Sign language and the Deaf community.* Silver Spring, MD: National Association of the Deaf.

Ball, C. (1995). Providing comprehensible input in a dead foreign language: Two text-based strategies. In J. Alatis, C. Straehle, B. Gallenberger, & M. Ronkin (Eds.), *Linguistics and the education of language teachers: Ethnolinguistic, psycholinguistic, and sociolinguistic aspects* (pp. 498-511). Washington, DC: Georgetown University Press.

Ball, S. (Ed.). (1990). *Foucault and education: Disciplines and knowledge.* London: Routledge.

Bamgbose, A., Banjo, A., & Thomas, A. (Eds.). (1997). *New Englishes: A West African perspective.* Trenton, NJ: Africa World Press.

Barber, C. (1993). *The English language: A historical introduction.* Cambridge, England: Cambridge University Press.

Baron, D. (1990). *The English-only question: An official language for Americans?* New Haven, CT: Yale University Press.

Bartolomé, L. (1998). *The misteaching of academic discourses: The politics of language in the classroom.* Boulder, CO: Westview Press.

Battison, R. (1978). *Lexical borrowing in American Sign Language.* Silver Spring, MD: Linstok Press.

Baugh, J. (2000). *Beyond Ebonics: Linguistic pride and racial prejudice.* Oxford, England: Oxford University Press.

Baynton, D. (1996). *Forbidden signs: American culture and the campaign against sign language.* Chicago: University of Chicago Press.

Benesch, S. (2001). *Critical English for academic purposes: Theory, politics, and practice.* Mahwah, NJ: Erlbaum.

Bernhardt, E. (1998). Sociohistorical perspectives on language teaching in the modern United States. In H. Byrnes (Ed.), *Learning foreign and second languages: Perspectives in research and scholarship* (pp. 39-57). New York: Modern Language Association.

Biehler, R., & Snowman, J. (1990). *Psychology applied to teaching* (6th ed.). Boston: Houghton Mifflin.

Blyth, C. (1997). A constructivist approach to grammar: Teaching teachers to teach aspect. *The Modern Language Journal, 81,* 50-66.

Bobaljik, J., Pensalfini, R., & Storto, L. (Eds.). (1996). *Papers on language endangerment and the maintenance of linguistic diversity.* Cambridge, MA: MIT Working Papers in Linguistics.

Bornstein, H. (Ed.). (1990). *Manual communication: Implications for education.* Washington, DC: Gallaudet University Press.

Boulter, C. (1997). Discourse and conceptual understanding in science. In B. Davies & D. Corson (Eds.), *Encyclopedia of language and education: Vol. 3. Oral discourse and education* (pp. 239-248). Dordrecht, The Netherlands: Kluwer.

Boulton, M. (1960). *Zamenhof: Creator of Esperanto.* London: Routledge & Kegan Paul.

Bourdieu, P., Passeron, J., & de Saint Martin, M. (1994). *Academic discourse.* Stanford, CA: Stanford University Press.

Bouvet, D. (1990). *The path to language: Bilingual education for deaf children.* Clevedon, England: Multilingual Matters.

Bowers, C. A. (1984). *The promise of theory: Education and the politics of cultural change.* New York: Longman.

Bransford, J., Brown, A., & Cocking, R. (Eds.). (2002). *How people learn: Brain, mind, experience, and school* (Expanded ed.). Washington, DC: Commission on Behavioral and Social Sciences and Education, National Academy Press.

Branson, J., & Miller, D. (2002). *Damned for their difference: The cultural construction of deaf people as disabled.* Washington, DC: Gallaudet University Press.

Brèe, G. (1984). The place of languages in the precollegiate humanities curriculum. In B. Ladner (Ed.), *The humanities in precollegiate education: Eighty-third Yearbook of the National Society for the Study of Education, Part II* (pp. 57-73). Chicago: University of Chicago Press.

Brosh, H. (1993). The influence of language status on language acquisition: Arabic in the Israeli setting. *Foreign Language Annals, 26,* 347-358.

Brown, C. (1995). The case for foreign languages. *Perspective: Council for Basic Education, 7,* 1-19.

Brutt-Griffler, J. (2002). *World English: A study of its development.* Clevedon, England: Multilingual Matters.

Brutt-Griffler, J., & Samimy, K. (1999). Revisiting the colonial in the postcolonial: Critical praxis for nonnative English-speaking teachers in a TESOL program. *TESOL Quarterly, 33,* 413-431.

Bunge, R. (1992). Language: The psyche of a people. In J. Crawford (Ed.), *Language loyalties* (pp. 376-380). Chicago: The University of Chicago Press.

Burrow, J. A., & Turville-Petre, T. (1996). *A book of Middle English* (2nd ed.). Oxford, England: Blackwell.

Byram, M. (1989). *Cultural studies in foreign language education.* Clevedon, England: Multilingual Matters.

Byram, M., Morgan, C., & Colleagues. (1994). *Teaching-and-learning language-and-culture.* Clevedon, England: Multilingual Matters.

Calvet, L. -J. (1999). *La guerre des langues et les politiques linguitiques* [Language wars and linguistic politics]. Paris: Hachette.

Calvet, L. -J. (2002). *Linguistique et colonialisme: Petit traité de glottophagie* [Linguistics and colonialism: A short treatise on glottophology]. Paris: Petite Biliothèque Payot.

Camp, W. (Ed.). (1990). *Camp's unfamiliar quotations from 2000 B.C. to the present.* Englewood Cliffs, NJ: Prentice-Hall.

Campbell, R., & Rosenthal, J. (2000). Heritage languages. In J. Rosenthal (Ed.), *Handbook of undergraduate second language education* (pp. 164-184). Mahwah, NJ: Erlbaum.

Canagarajah, A. S. (1999). *Resisting linguistic imperialism in English teaching.* Oxford, England: Oxford University Press.

Carter, R. (Ed.). (1990). *Knowledge about language and the curriculum: The LINC Reader.* London: Hodder & Stoughton.

Carter, R. (1998). *Mapping the mind.* Berkeley: University of California Press.

Chamberlain, C., Morford, J., & Mayberry, R. (Eds.). (2000). *Language acquisition by eye.* Mahwah, NJ: Erlbaum.

Chambliss, J. J. (1987). *Educational theory as theory of conduct: From Aristotle to Dewey.* Albany: State University of New York Press.

Chastain, K. (1976). *Developing second-language skills: Theory to practice* (2nd ed.). Chicago: Rand McNally.

Chomsky, N. (1975). *Reflections on language.* New York: Pantheon.

Chomsky, N. (1993). Mental constructions and social reality. In E. Reuland & W. Abraham (Eds.), *Knowledge and language: Vol. 1. From Orwell's problem to Plato's problem* (pp. 29-58). Dordrecht, The Netherlands: Kluwer.

Chomsky, N. (1994). Chomsky, Noam. In S. Suttenplan (Ed.), *A companion to the philosophy of mind* (pp. 153-167). Oxford, England: Blackwell.

Chomsky, N. (2000). *New horizons in the study of language and mind.* Cambridge, England: Cambridge University Press.

Cobb, P. (1994). Where is the mind? Constructivist and socioculturalist perspectives on mathematical development. *Educational Researcher, 23*, 13-20.

Cobb, P. (1996). Where is the mind? A coordination of sociocultural and cognitive constructionist perspectives. In C. Fosnot (Ed.), *Constructivism: Theory, perspectives, and practice* (pp. 34-52). New York: Teachers College Press.

Cobern, W. (1993). Contextual constructivism: The impact of culture on the learning and teaching of science. In K. Tobin (Ed.), *The practice of constructivism in science education* (pp. 51-69). Hillsdale, NJ: Erlbaum.

Condon, M., Clyde, J., Kyle, D., & Hovda, R. (1993). A constructivist basis for teaching and teacher education: A framework for program development and research on graduates. *Journal of Teacher Education, 44*, 273-278.

Confrey, J. (1995). How compatible are radical constructivism, sociocultural approaches, and social constructivism? In L. Steffe & J. Gale (Eds.), *Constructivism in education* (pp. 185-225). Hillsdale, NJ: Erlbaum.

Conroy, J. (1994). *Beginner's Esperanto: Esperanto por komencantoj.* New York: Hippocrene.

Cook, V., & Newson, M. (1996). *Chomsky's universal grammar: An introduction* (2nd ed.). Oxford, England: Blackwell.

Cooper, J. (1993). *Literacy: Helping children construct meaning* (2nd ed.). Boston: Houghton Mifflin.

Cooper, R. (1989). *Language planning and social change.* Cambridge, England: Cambridge University Press.

Cornforth, F. (1957). *Plato's theory of knowledge.* New York: Liberal Arts Press.

Corsetti, R., Pinto, M., & Tolomeo, M. (2004). Regularizing the regular: The phenomenon of overregularization in Esperanto-speaking children. *Language Problems and Language Planning, 28,* 261-282.

Corson, D. (1993). *Language, minority education and gender.* Clevedon, England: Multilingual Matters.

Corson, D. (1999). *Language policy in schools: A resource for teachers and administrators.* Mahwah, NJ: Erlbaum.

Corson, D. (2001). *Language diversity and education.* Mahwah, NJ: Erlbaum.

Coulombe, P. (1993). Language rights, individual and communal. *Language Problems and Language Planning, 17,* 140-152.

Craig, B. (1995). Boundary discourse and the authority of language in the second-language classroom: A social-constructivist approach. In J. Alatis, C. Straehle, B. Gallenberger, & M. Ronkin (Eds.), *Georgetown University round table on languages and linguistics 1995: Linguistics and the education of language teachers* (pp. 40-54). Washington, DC: Georgetown University Press.

Crawford, J. (1992a). *Hold your tongue: Bilingualism and the politics of "English only."* Reading, MA: Addison-Wesley.

Crawford, J. (Ed.). (1992b). *Language loyalties: A source book on the official English controversy.* Chicago: University of Chicago Press.

Cresswell, J., & Hartley, J. (1992). *Esperanto: A complete course for beginners* (Rev. ed.). Lincolnwood, IL: NTC Publishing Group.

Crookall, D., & Oxford, R. (1988). Review essay. *Language Learning, 31,* 128-140.

Crookes, G., Sakka, R., Shiroma, S., & Ye, L. (1991). *Towards a generic curriculum for the less commonly taught languages.* (Research Note #1). Honolulu: University of Hawai'i, Second Language Teaching and Curriculum Center.

Crystal, D. (1987). *The Cambridge encyclopedia of language.* Cambridge, England: Cambridge University Press.

Crystal, D. (2000). *Language death.* Cambridge, England: Cambridge University Press.

Crystal, D. (2003). *English as a global language* (2nd ed.). Cambridge, England: Cambridge University Press.

Curtain, H., & Pesola, C. (1994). *Languages and children, making the match: Foreign language instruction for an early start, grades K-8* (2nd ed.). White Plains, NY: Longman.

Dalby, A. (2003). *Language in danger: The loss of linguistic diversity and the threat to our future.* New York: Columbia University Press.

Davis, J., & Osborn, T. (2003). *The language teacher's portfolio: A guide for professional development.* Westport, CT: Praeger.

Davis, R., Maher, C., & Noddings, N. (Eds.). (1990). *Constructivist views on the teaching and learning of mathematics.* Reston, VA: National Council of Teachers of Mathematics.

Dearden, R., Hirst, P., & Peters, R. S. (Eds.). (1972). *Education and the development of reason.* London: Routledge and Kegan Paul.

Delpit, L., & Dowdy, J. (Eds.). (2002). *The skin that we speak: Thoughts on language and culture in the classroom.* New York: New Press.

DiPietro, R. (1971). *Language structures in contrast.* Rowley, MA: Newbury House.

Dively, V., Metzger, M., Taub, S., & Baer, A. (Eds.). (2001). *Signed languages: Discoveries from international research.* Washington, DC: Gallaudet University Press.

Division of Psychology, Institute of Educational Research, Teachers College, Columbia University. (1933). *Language learning: Summary of a Report to the International Auxilary Language Association in the United States.* New York: Bureau of Publications, Teachers College, Columbia University.

Dixon, R. M. W. (1997). *The rise and fall of languages.* Cambridge, England: Cambridge University Press.

Dodge, E. (1941). Esperanto: Instrument of mental training. *Education, 61,* 301-317.

Dorian, N. (1998). Western language ideologies and small-language prospects. In L. Grenoble & L. Whaley (Eds.), *Endangered languages: Current issues and future prospects* (pp. 3-21). Cambridge, England: Cambridge University Press.

Draper, J., & Hicks, J. (1996). Foreign language enrollments in public secondary schools, Fall 1994: Summary report. *Foreign Language Annals, 29,* 303-314.

Driver, R., Asoko, H., Leach, J., Mortimer, E., & Scott, P. (1994). Constructing scientific knowledge in the classroom. *Educational Researcher, 23,* 5-12.

Duerr, H. P. (Ed.). (1980). *Versuchungen Aufsätze zur Philosophie Paul Feyerabends: Vol. 1* [Exploratory essays on the philosophy of Paul Feyerabend: Vol. 1]. Frankfurt, Germany: Suhrkamp Verlag.

Duerr, H. P. (Ed.). (1981). *Versuchungen Aufsätze zur Philosophie Paul Feyerabends: Vol. 2* [Exploratory essays on the philosophy of Paul Feyerabend: Vol. 2]. Frankfurt, Germany: Suhrkamp Verlag.

Duffy, T., & Jonassen, D. (Eds.). (1992). *Constructivism and the technology of instruction: A conversation.* Hillsdale, NJ: Erlbaum.

Dulay, H., Burt, M., & Krashen, S. (1982). *Language two.* New York: Oxford University Press.

Duliĉenko, A. (1988). Проекты всеобщих и международных языков (Universal and international language projects). *Interlinguistica Tartuensis, 5,* 126-162.

Duliĉenko, A. (1989). Интерлингвистика: Сущность и проблемы (Interlinguistics: Essence and problems). *Interlinguistica Tartuensis, 6,* 18-41.

Durand, C. (2001). *La mise en place des monopoles du savoir* [The placement and position of monopolies of knowledge]. Paris: L'Harmattan.

Eco, U. (1995). *The search for the perfect language.* Oxford: Blackwell.

Edwards, Jane. (1986). Esperanto and an international research context. In H. Tonkin & K. Johnson-Weiner (Eds.), *The idea of a universal language* (pp. 97-107). New York: Center for Research and Documentation on World Language Problems.

Edwards, Jane. (1993). Esperanto as an international research context. In I. Richmond (Ed.), *Aspects of internationalism: Language and culture* (pp. 21-34). Lanham, MD: University Press of America, in conjunction with the Center for Research and Documentation on World Language Problems.

Edwards, John. (1994). *Multilingualism.* London: Routledge.

Edwards, John. (1996). Language and society in a changing world. InT. Hickey & J. Williams (Eds.), *Language, education and society in a changing world* (pp. 29-

37). Dublin: Irish Association for Applied Linguistics and Multilingual Matters.
Ehrenreich, S. (2003). Abroad and back home: How can foreign language teacher education help develop intercultural competence? In R. Tormey (Ed.), *Teaching social justice* (pp. 161-172). Limerick: Center for Educational Disadvantage Research, Mary Immaculate College, and Ireland Aid.
Elgin, S. (2000). *The language imperative.* Cambridge, MA: Perseus Books.
Elvin, L. (1977). *The place of commonsense in educational thought.* London: George Allen & Unwin.
Emmorey, K. (2002). *Language, cognition, and the brain: Insights from sign language research.* Mahwah, NJ: Erlbaum.
Emmorey, K. (Ed.). (2003). *Perspectives on classifier constructions in sign languages.* Mahwah, NJ: Erlbaum.
Emmorey, K., & Lane, H. (Eds.). (2000). *The signs of language revisited: An anthology to honor Ursula Bellugi and Edward Klima.* Mahwah, NJ: Erlbaum.
Emmorey, K., & Reilly, J. (Eds.). (1995a). *Language, gesture, and space.* Hillsdale, NJ: Erlbaum.
Emmorey, K., & Reilly, J. (1995b). Theoretical issues related language, gesture, and space: An overview. In K. Emmorey & J. Reilly (Eds.), *Language, gesture, and space* (pp. 1-16). Hillsdale, NJ: Erlbaum.
Erting, C. (1978). Language policy and deaf ethnicity in the United States. *Sign Language Studies, 19,* 139-152.
Erting, C. (1985). Cultural conflict in a school for deaf children. *Anthropology and Education Quarterly, 16,* 225-243.
Esperanto League for North American and the California Esperanto Education Commission. (1988). *Esperanto handbook for teachers: Guide to the international language.* El Cerrito, CA: Author.
Everson, M. (1993). Research in the less commonly taught languages. In A. Omaggio Hadley (Ed.), *Research in language learning: Principles, processes, and prospects* (pp. 198-228). Lincolnwood, IL: National Textbook Company, in conjunction with the American Council on the Teaching of Foreign Languages.
Fairclough, N. (1989). *Language and power.* London: Longman.
Fairclough, N. (Ed.). (1992). *Critical language awareness.* London: Longman.
Fairclough, N. (1995). *Critical discourse analysis: The critical study of language.* London: Longman.
Faltis, C. (1997). Bilingual education in the United States. In J. Cummins & D. Corson (Eds.), *Encyclopedia of language and education: Vol. 5. Bilingual education* (pp. 189-197). Dordrecht, The Netherlands: Kluwer.
Fantini, A., & Reagan, T. (1992). *Esperanto and education: Toward a research agenda.* Washington, DC: Esperantic Studies Foundation.
Fensham, P., Gunstone, R., & White, R. (Eds.). (1994). *The content of science: A constructivist approach to its teaching and learning.* London: Falmer Press.
Fettes, M. (2001). Les géostratégies de l'interlingualisme [The geostrategies of interlingualism]. *Terminogramme, 99/100,* 35-46.

Fettes, M. (2003a). The geostrategies of interlingualism. In J. Maurais & M. Morris (Eds.), *Languages in a globalising world* (pp. 37-46). Cambridge, England: Cambridge University Press.

Fettes, M. (2003b). Interlingualism: A world-centric approach to language policy and planning. In H. Tonkin & T. Reagan (Eds.), *Language in the 21st century* (pp. 47-58). Amsterdam: John Benjamins.

Feyerabend, P. (1978). *Against method: Outline of an anarchistic theory of knowledge.* London: Verso.

Feyerabend, P. (1987). *Farewell to reason.* London: Verso.

Feyerabend, P. (1991). *Three dialogues on knowledge.* Oxford, England: Blackwell.

Feyerabend, P. (1993). *Against* method (3rd ed.). London: Verso.

Fink-Eitel, H. (1988). *Foucault zur einführung* [Foucault: An introduction]. Hamburg, Germany: Verlag GmbH (Hamburg).

Fischer, R., & Lane, H. (Eds.). (1993). *Looking back: A reader on the history of deaf communities and their sign languages.* Hamburg, Germany: Signum Press.

Fisher, A. (1921). Modern languages by way of Esperanto. *Modern Languages, 2,* 179-182.

Forman, G., & Pufall, P. (Eds.). (1988). *Constructivism in the computer age.* Hillsdale, NJ: Erlbaum.

Forster, P. (1982). *The Esperanto movement.* The Hague, The Netherlands: Mouton.

Forster, P. (1987). Some social sources of resistance to Esperanto. In *Serta Gratvlatoria in Honorem Juan Régulo, II (Esperantismo)* (pp. 203-211). La Laguna, Spain: University de La Laguna.

Fosnot, C. (1993). Preface. In J. Brooks & M. Brooks, *The case for constructivist classrooms* (pp. vii-viii). Alexandria, VA: Association for Supervision and Curriculum Development.

Fosnot, C. (Ed.). (1996a). *Constructivism: Theory, perspectives, and practice.* New York: Teachers College Press.

Fosnot, C. (1996b). Constructivism: A psychological theory of learning. In C. Fosnot (Ed.), *Constructivism: Theory, perspectives, and practice* (pp. 8-33). New York: Teachers College Press.

Foucault, M. (1970). *The order of things: An archeaology of the human sciences.* New York: Vintage.

Foucault, M. (1972). *The archaeology of knowledge and the discourse on language.* New York: Harper & Row.

Foucault, M. (1973). *The birth of the clinic: An archeaology of medical perception.* New York: Vintage.

Foucault, M. (1975). *Surveiller et punir: Naissance de la prison* [Discipline and punishment: The birth of the prison]. Paris: Gallimard.

Frank, H. (1976). Malonga enkonduko en la kibernetikan pedagogion/Kurze Einfuehrung in die Kybernetische Pädagogik [A short introduction to pedagogical cybernetics]. In H. Behrmann & S. Stimec (Eds.), *Bildung und Berechnung/Klerigo kaj prikalkulado* [Education and calculation] (pp. 9-55). Alsbach, Germany: Leuchtturn-Verlag.

Frank, H. (1978). Grundlagen und sprachpädagogische Anwendung einer informationstheoretischen Transferanalyse [Underpinnings and language pedagogy applications of an information theory transfer analysis]. *Grundlogenstudien aus Kybernetik und Geisteswissenschaft, 19,* 75-88.

Frank, H. (1987a). Propedeutika valoro de la internacia lingvo: Kibernetika teorio kaj empiriaj rezultoj de la lingvo-orientiga instruado de la Internacia Lingvo kiel bazo de pli posta lernado de etnaj lingvoj [The propaedeutic value of the international language: Cybernetic theory and empirical results of the language-orientation teaching of the International Language as a basis for subsequent learning of ethnic language]. In *Serta Gratvlatoria in Honorem Juan Régulo, II (Esperantismo)* (pp. 213-222). La Laguna, Spain: University de La Laguna.

Frank, H. (1987b). Wartosc propedeutyczna języka międzynarodowego [Propaedeutic effects of the international language]. *Międzynardoowa komunikacja językowa/Internacia lingva komunikado: Materialy konferencyjne — IV* [International linguistic communication: Conference materials] (pp. 124-136). Lódź: Uniwersytet Lódzki, Zrzeszenie Studentow Polskich, Studenckie Kolo Naukowe Esperantystów.

Frank, H., & Barandovska, V. (1991). Lernpliffaciligo pro antaumetitaj lingvokursoj [Increased ease of learning as a result of language courses]. *Internacia Pedagogia Revuo, 21,* 11-15.

Fromkin, V., & Rodman, R. (1993). *An introduction to language* (5th ed.). Fort Worth, TX: Harcourt Brace Jovanovich.

Gardner, R. (1985). *Social psychology and language learning: The role of attitudes and motivation.* London: Edward Arnold.

Geisler, E. (1979). La unuaj mezuradoj pri la lernfaciligo internacia kaj angla lingvoj [Initial results on the ease of learning the international language and English]. *Europa Dokumentaro, 21,* 9-10.

Gergen, K. (1982). *Towards transformation in social knowledge.* New York: Springer-Verlag.

Gergen, K. (1995). Social construction and the educational process. In L. Steffe & J. Gale (Eds.), *Constructivism in education* (pp. 17-39). Hillsdale, NJ: Erlbaum.

Gledhill, C. (2000). *The grammar of Esperanto: A corpus-based description* (2nd ed.). Muechen, Germany: Lincom Europa.

Glossop, R. (1988). International child-to-child correspondence using Esperanto. *Gifted International, 5,* 81-84.

Glossop, R. (1991, December 13). How to integrate language study and global education. Paper presented at the tenth annual Conference on Language and Communication, New York City.

Gold, D. (1980). Towards a study of possible Yiddish and Hebrew influence on Esperanto. In I. Szerdahelyi (Ed.), *Miscellanea interlinguistica* (pp. 300-367). Budapest, Hungary: Tankönyvkiadó.

Gold, D. (1982). Pli pri judaj aspektoj de Esperanto [On the Jewish aspects of Esperanto]. *Planlingvistiko, 1,* 7-14.

Golden, B. (1997). Conservation of the heritage of Volapüp. In H. Tonkin (Ed.), *Esperanto, interlinguistics, and planned languages* (pp. 183-189). Lanham, MD: University Press of America.

Gollnick, D., & Chinn, P. (1994). *Multicultural education in a pluralistic society* (4th ed.). New York: Merrill.

Gomes de Matos, F. (1995). The linguistic rights of language learners. *Language Planning Newsletter, 11*, 1-2.

Goodman, T. (1978). Esperanto: Threat or ally? *Foreign Language Annals, 11*, 201-203.

Graddol, D. (1998). *The future of English.* London: The British Council.

Green, L. (2002). *African American English: A linguistic introduction.* Cambridge, England: Cambridge University Press.

Gregor, D. (1976). Der kulturelle Wert des Esperanto [The cultural world of Esperanto]. In R. Haupenthal (Ed.), *Plansprachen: Beitraege zur Interlinguistik* (pp. 297-304). Darmstad, Germany: Wissenschaftliche Buchgesellschaft.

Grennon Brooks, J., & Brooks, M. (1993). *The case for constructivist classrooms.* Alexandria, VA: Association for Supervision and Curriculum Development.

Grenoble, L., & Whaley, L. (Eds.). (1998a). *Endangered languages: Current issues and future prospects.* Cambridge, England: Cambridge University Press.

Grenoble, L., & Whaley, L. (Eds.). (1998b).Toward a typology of language endangerment. In *Endangered languages* (pp. 22-54). Cambridge, England: Cambridge University Press.

Grin, F. (1993). European economic integration and the fate of lesser-used languages. *Language Problems and Language Planning, 17*, 101-116.

Grove, C. (2003). The role of instruction in Spanish second language acquisition. In B. Lafford & R. Salaberry (Eds.), *Spanish second language acquisition: State of the science* (pp. 287-319). Washington, DC: Georgetown University Press.

Grube, G. M. A. (1980). *Plato's thought.* Indianapolis, IN: Hackett.

Guerard, A. (1922). *A short history of the international language movement.* London: T. F. Unwin.

Gunnarsson, B. (1997). Language for special purposes. In G. Tucker & D. Corson (Eds.), *Encyclopedia of language and education: Vol. 4. Second language education* (pp. 105-117). Dordrecht, The Netherlands: Kluwer.

Gunnarsson, B., Linell, P., & Nordberg, B. (Eds.). (1997). *The construction of professional discourse.* London: Longman.

Gustason, G., & Zawolkow, E. (1993). *Signing Exact English.* Los Alamitos, CA: Modern Signs Press.

Gutmann, A. (1987). *Democratic education.* Princeton, NJ: Princeton University Press.

Hafernik, J., Messerschmitt, D., & Vandrick, S. (2002). *Ethical issues for ESL faculty: Social justice in practice.* Mahwah, NJ: Erlbaum.

Hagège, C. (1996). *Le français: Histoire d'un combat* [French: History of a struggle]. Paris: Éditions Michel Hagège.

Hagège, C. (2000). *Halte à la mort des langues* [An end to language death]. Paris: Éditions Odile Jacob.

Hahn, H. (1986). Public support for rehabilitation programs: The analysis of U.S. disability policy. *Disability, Handicap and Society, 1*, 121-137.

Hale, K. (1998). On endangered languages and the importance of linguistic diversity. In L. Grenoble & L. Whaley (Eds.), *Endangered languages: Current issues and future prospects* (pp. 192-216). Cambridge, England: Cambridge University Press.

Hall, J. K. (2001). *Methods for teaching foreign languages: Creating a community of learners in the classroom.* Upper Saddle River, NJ: Merrill Prentice Hall.

Hall, J. K., & Eggington, W. (Eds.). (2000). *The sociopolitics of English language teaching.* Clevedon, England: Multilingual Matters.

Halloran, J. (1952). A four year experiment in Esperanto as an introduction to French. *British Journal of Educational Psychology, 22,* 200-204.

Hana, J. (1998). *Two-level morphology of Esperanto.* Unpublished doctoral thesis, Charles University, Prague.

Haugen, E. (1987). *Blessings of Babel: Bilingualism and language planning.* Berlin, Germany: Mouton de Gruyter.

Hawkes, T. (1977). *Structuralism and semiotics.* Berkeley: University of California Press.

Hawkins, E. (1981). *Modern languages in the curriculum.* Cambridge, England: Cambridge University Press.

Henning, E. (1995). Problematising the discourse of classroom management from the view of social constructivism. *South African Journal of Education, 15,* 124-129.

Herman, D. (2002). "Our patriotic duty": Insights from professional history, 1890-1920. In T. Osborn (Ed.), *The future of foreign language education in the United States* (pp. 1-29). Westport, CT: Bergin & Garvey.

Hernández-Chávez, E. (1995). Language policy in the United States: A history of cultural genocide. In T. Skutnabb-Kangas & R. Phillipson, in conjunction with M. Rannut (Eds.), *Linguistic human rights: Overcoming linguistic discrimination* (pp. 141-158). Berlin, Germany: Mouton de Gruyter.

Herriman, M., & Burnaby, B. (Eds.). (1996). *Language policies in English-dominant countries.* Clevedon, England: Multilingual Matters.

Hertzfeld, A., & Lastra, Y. (Eds.). (1999). *Las causas sociales de la desaparición y del mantenimento de las lenguas en las naciones de América* [The social causes of the disappearance and maintenance of languages in the Americas]. Hermosillo: Unisón.

Hindley, R. (1990). *The death of the Irish language.* London: Routledge.

Hirst, P. (1974). *Knowledge and the curriculum.* London: Routledge & Kegan Paul.

Hirst, P., & Peters, R. S. (1970). *The logic of education.* London: Routledge & Kegan Paul.

Hitler, A. (1940). *Mein Kampf: Complete and unabridged.* New York: Reynal & Hitchcock.

Holborow, M. (1999). *The politics of English: A Marxist view of language.* London: Sage.

Hymes, D. (1996). *Ethnography, linguistics, narrative inequality: Toward an understanding of voice.* London: Taylor and Francis.

Ihde, T. (1997). Teacher certification and less commonly taught languages. *Journal of Celtic Language Learning, 3,* 41-50.

Jacobs, R. (1996). Just how hard is it to learn ASL? The case for ASL as a truly foreign language. In C. Lucas (Ed.), *Multicultural aspects of sociolinguistics in deaf communities* (pp. 183-226). Washington, DC: Gallaudet University Press.

James, C., & Garrett, P. (1992). *Language awareness in the classroom.* London: Longman.

James, C. V. (1979). Foreign languages in the school curriculum. In G. E. Perren (Ed.), *Foreign languages in education* (pp. 7-28). London: CILT.

Janks, H. (1991). A critical approach to the teaching of language. *Educational Review, 43,* 191-199.

Janks, H. (1997). Critical discourse analysis as a research tool. *Discourse: Studies in the Politics of Education, 18,* 329-342.

Janks, H., & Ivanic, R. (1992). Critical language awareness. In N. Fairclough (Ed.), *Critical language awareness* (pp. 305-331). London: Longman.

Janse, M., & Tol, S. (Eds.). (2003). *Language death and language maintenance.* Amsterdam: John Benjamins.

Janton, P. (1988). *Esperanto: Lingvo, literaturo, movado.* Rotterdam, The Netherlands: Universala Esperanto-Asocio.

Janton, P. (1993). *Esperanto: Language, literature, and community* (H. Tonkin, Ed., H. Tonkin, J. Edwards, & K. Johnson-Weiner, Trans.). Albany: State University Press of New York.

Jarvis, G. (1980). The value of second-language learning. In F. Grittner (Ed.) *Learning a second language: Seventy-Ninth Yearbook of the National Society for the Study of Education* (pp. 26-43). Chicago: University of Chicago Press.

Jensen, E. (1998). *Teaching with the brain in mind.* Alexandria, VA: Association for Supervision and Curriculum Development.

Johnson, B. (2003). *Values in English language teaching.* Mahwah, NJ: Erlbaum.

Johnson, R., Liddell, S., & Erting, C. (1989). *Unlocking the curriculum: Principles for achieving access in deaf education* (Gallaudet Research Institute Working Paper 89-3). Washington, DC: Gallaudet University.

Jordan, D. (1992). *Being colloquial in Esperanto: A reference guide for Americans.* Lanham, MD: University Press of America.

Jordan, D. (1997). Esperanto and Esperantism: Symbols and motivations in a movement for linguistic equality. In H. Tonkin (Ed.) *Esperanto, interlinguistics, and planned language* (pp. 38-65). Lanham, MD: University Press of America, in conjunction with the Center for Research and Documentation on World Language Problems.

Jordan, E., & Walton, A. R. (1987). Truly foreign languages: Instructional challenges. *Annals of the American Academy of Social and Political Science, 490,* 110-124.

Kachru, B. (Ed.). (1982). *The other tongue: English across cultures.* Oxford, England: Pergamon Press.

Kafai, Y., & Resnick, M. (Eds.). (1996). *Constructivism in practice: Designing, thinking, and learning in a digital world.* Mahwah, NJ: Erlbaum.

Kalocsay, K. (1963). *Lingvo, stilo, formo* [Language, style, form]. Budapest, Hungary: Librejo Pirato. (Orginal work published 1931)

Kalocsay, K., & Waringhien, G. (1985). *Plena analiza gramatiko de Esperanto* [A short analytic grammar of Esperanto] (5th ed.). Rotterdam, The Netherlands: Universala Esperanto-Asocio.

Kamii, C., Manning, M., & Manning, G. (Eds.). (1991). *Early literacy: A constructivist foundation for whole language.* Washington, DC: National Education Association.

Kannapell, B. (1993). *Language choice, language identity: A sociolinguistic study of deaf college students.* Burtonsville, MD: Linstok Press.

Kanpol, B. (1994). *Critical pedagogy: An introduction.* Westport, CT: Bergin & Garvey.

Kaplan, R., & Baldauf, R. B. (1997). *Language planning: From practice to theory.* Clevedon, England: Multilingual Matters.

Karabel, J., & Halsey, A. (Eds.). (1977). *Power and ideology in education.* New York: Oxford University Press.

Karier, C. (1986). *Scientists of the mind: Intellectual founders of modern psychology.* Urbana: University of Illinois Press.

Kaufman, D., & Grennon Brooks, J. (1996). Interdisciplinary collaboration in teacher education: A constructivist approach. *TESOL Quarterly, 30,* 231-251.

Knowlson, J. (1975). *Universal language schemes in England and France, 1600-1800.* Toronto, Canada: University of Toronto Press.

Kolker, B. (1988). Вклад русского языка в лексику эсперанто. (The contribution of the Russian language to the lexicon of Esperanto). *Interlinguistica Tartuensis, 5,* 74-91.

Kontra, M., Phillipson, R., Skutnabb-Kangas, T., & Várady, T. (Eds.). (1999). *Language: A right and a resource—Approaching linguistic human rights.* Budapest, Hungary: Central European University Press.

Krashen, S. (1981). *Second language acquisition and second language learning.* Oxford, England: Pergamon.

Krashen, S. (1982). *Principles and practices of second language acquisition.* Oxford, England: Pergamon.

Krashen, S. (1985). *The input hypothesis: Issues and implications.* London: Longman.

Krauss, M. (1992). The world's languages in crisis. *Language, 68,* 4-10.

Kubota, R., Austin, T., & Saito-Abbott, Y. (2003). Diversity and inclusion of sociopolitical issues in foreign language classrooms: An exploratory survey. *Foreign Language Annals, 36,* 12-24.

Kuhn, T. (1996). *The structure of scientific revolutions* (3rd ed.). Chicago: University of Chicago Press. (Original work published 1962)

Kumaravadivelu, B. (1994). The postmethod condition: (E)merging strategies for second/foreign language teaching. *TESOL Quarterly, 28,* 27-48.

Kuznetsov, S. (1988). Фонологическая система эсперано. (The phonological system of Esperanto). *Interlinguistica Tartuensis, 5,* 25-52.

Kyle, J., & Woll, B. (1985). *Sign language: The study of Deaf people and their language.* Cambridge, England: Cambridge University Press.

Lafayette, R. (Ed.). (1996). *National standards: A catalyst for reform.* Lincolnwood, IL: National Textbook Co., in conjunction with the American Council on the Teaching of Foreign Languages.

Lakoff, G., & Johnson, M. (1980). *Metaphors we live by.* Chicago: The University of Chicago Press.

Lampe, J. (2000). *Yugoslavia as history: Twice there was a country* (2nd ed.). Cambridge, England: Cambridge University Press.

Lane, H. (1992). *The mask of benevolence: Disabling the deaf community.* New York: Alfred A. Knopf.

Lane, H., Hoffmeister, R., & Bahan, B. (1996). *A journey into the deaf-world.* San Diego, CA: DawnSign Press.

Large, A. (1985). *The artificial language movement.* Oxford, England: Basil Blackwell.

Lee, P. (1996). *The Whorf theory complex: A critical reconstruction.* Philadelphia: John Benjamins.

Leith, D. (1997). *A social history of English* (2nd ed.). London: Routledge.

Leon-Smith, G. (1987). *The role of Esperanto in the teaching of modern languages.* London: Esperanto-Asocio de Britujo.

Liddell, S. (1995). Real, surrogate, and token space: Grammatical consequences in ASL. In K. Emmorey & J. Reilly (Eds.), *Language, gesture, and space* (pp. 19-41). Hillsdale, NJ: Erlbaum.

Liddell, S. (2003). *Grammar, gesture, and meaning in American Sign Language.* Cambridge, England: Cambridge University Press.

Lins, U. (1980). *La danĝera lingvo.* Moscow: Progreso.

Lippi-Green, R. (2000). That's not my language: The struggle to (re)define African American English. In R. González & I. Melis (Eds.), *Language ideologies: Critical perspectives on the Official English Movement* (Vol. 1, pp. 230-247). Mahwah, NJ: Erlbaum, in conjunction with the National Council of Teachers of English.

Lipton, G. (1992). *Practical handbook to elementary foreign language programs* (2nd ed.). Lincolnwood, IL: National Textbook.

Liskin-Gasparro, J. (1982). *ETS oral proficiency testing manual.* Princeton, NJ: Educational Testing Service.

Littlewood, W. (1984). *Foreign and second language learning: Language acquisition research and its implications for the classroom.* Cambridge, England: Cambridge University Press.

Liu, J. (1999). Non-native-English-speaking professionals in TESOL. *TESOL Quarterly, 33,* 85-102.

Loeb, A. (Ed.). (1996). *The wit and wisdom of Mark Twain.* New York: Barnes & Noble Books.

Lo Jacomo, F. (1981). *Liberté ou autorité dans l'évolution de l'espéranto* [Liberty or authority in the evolution of Esperanto]. Paris: Author.

Lomas, C., & Osoro, A. (Eds.). (1993). *El enfoque comunicativo de la enseñanza de la lengua.* Buenos Aires, Argentina: Paidós.

Lubiner, E. (1996). *Learning about languages: A comprehensive FLEX activity book.* Lincolnwood, IL: National Textbook.

Lucas, C. (Ed.). (1989). *The sociolinguistics of the deaf community.* San Diego, CA: Academic Press.

Lucas, C. (Ed.). (1995). *Sociolinguistics in deaf communities.* Washington, DC: Gallaudet University Press.

Lucas, C. (Ed.). (1996). *Multicultural aspects of sociolinguistics in deaf communities.* Washington, DC: Gallaudet University Press.

Lucas, C. (Ed.). (2001). *The sociolinguistics of sign languages.* Cambridge, England: Cambridge University Press.

Lucas, C., Bayley, R., & Valli, C. (2001). *Sociolinguistic variation in American Sign Language.* Washington, DC: Gallaudet University Press.

Lucas, C., & Valli, C. (1989). Language contact in the American Deaf community. In C. Lucas (Ed.), *The sociolinguistics of the deaf community* (pp. 11-40). San Diego, CA: Academic Press.

Lucas, C., & Valli, C. (1991). ASL or contact signing: Issues of judgement. *Language in Society, 20,* 201-216.

Lucas, C., & Valli, C. (1992). *Language contact in the American deaf community.* San Diego: Academic Press.

Mackey, W. (2003). Forecasting the fate of languages. In J. Maurais & M. Morris (Eds.), *Languages in a globalising world* (pp. 64-81). Cambridge, England: Cambridge University Press.

MacMillan, M. (1982). Henri Bourassa on the defence of language rights. *Dalhousie Review, 62,* 413-430.

Magadla, L. (1996). Constructivism: A practitioner's perspective. *South African Journal of Higher Education, 10,* 83-88.

Markarian, R. (1964). *The educational value of Esperanto teaching in the schools.* Rotterdam, The Netherlands: Universala Esperanto-Asocio.

Martin-Jones, M., & Romaine, S. (1986). Semilingualism: A half-baked theory of communicative competence. *Applied Linguistics, 7,* 26-38.

Matthews, S., & Yip, V. (1994). *Cantonese: A comprehensive grammar.* London: Routledge.

Maxwell, D. (1988). On the acquisition of Esperanto. *Studies in Second Language Acquisition, 10,* 51-61.

McArthur, T. (1998). *The English languages.* Cambridge, England: Cambridge University Press.

McKay, S., & Hornberger, N. (Eds.). (1996). *Sociolinguistics and language teaching.* Cambridge, England: Cambridge University Press.

McRae, K. (1978). Bilingual language districts in Finland and Canada: Adventures in the transplanting of an institution. *Canadian Public Policy, 4,* 331-351.

McWhorter, J. (1998). *The word on the street: Fact and fable about American English.* London: Plenum Trade.

Measures, E., Quell, C., & Wells, G. (1997). A sociocultural perspective on classroom discourse. In B. Davies & D. Corson (Eds.), *Encyclopedia of language and education: Vol. 3. Oral discourse and education* (pp. 21-29). Dordrecht, The Netherlands: Kluwer.

Meder, B. (1978). Efikoj de la lingvo-orientiga instruado al la lernsukceso en la mezgrada lernejo [The effects of the language-orientation instruction to the learning success of small languages]. *Europa dokumentaro, 20,* 15-18.

Meinhardt, G. (1978). Latent knowledge of vocabulary of the international language, arising from one's native language. *Europa dokumentaro, 18,* 13-15.

Meier, R. (1990). Person deixis in American Sign Language. In S. Fischer & P. Siple (Eds.), *Theoretical issues in sign language research: Volume 1. Linguistics* (pp. 175-190). Chicago: University of Chicago Press.

Merquior, J. G. (1985). *Foucault.* Berkeley: University of California Press.

Merrill, M. (1992). Constructivism and instructional design. In T. Duffy & D. Jonassen (Eds.), *Constructivism and the technology of instruction: A conversation* (pp. 99-114). Hillsdale, NJ: Erlbaum.

Met, M., & Galloway, V. (1992). Research in foreign language curriculum. In P. Jackson (Ed.), *Handbook of research on curriculum* (pp. 852-890). New York: Macmillan.

Metzger, M. (Ed.). (2000). *Bilingualism and identity in deaf communities.* Washington, DC: Gallaudet University Press.

Mintzes, J., Wandersee, J., & Novak, J. (Eds.). (1997). *Teaching science for understanding: A human constructivist view.* San Diego, CA: Academic Press.

Mitchell, B., & Robinson, F. (1992). *A guide to Old English* (5th ed.). Oxford, England: Blackwell.

Moll, L. (Ed.). (1990). *Vygotsky and education: Instructional implications and applications of sociocultural psychology.* Cambridge, England: Cambridge University Press.

Moore, J. (1980). The structure of Esperanto. *Babel: Journal of the Australian Federation of Modern Language Teacher's Association, 16,* 25-27.

Mufwene, S., Rickford, J., Bailey, G., & Baugh, J. (Eds.). (1998). *African-American English: Structure, history and use.* London: Routledge.

Munnik, A. (1994). *Learn Xhosa.* Pietermaritzburg, South Africa: Shuter & Shooter.

Nash, J. (1987). Policy and practice in the American Sign Language community. *International Journal of the Sociology of Language, 68,* 7-22.

Neidle, C., Kegl, J., Maclaughlin, D., Bahan, B., & Lee, R. (2000). *The syntax of American Sign Language: Functional categories and hierarchical structure.* Cambridge, MA: MIT Press.

Neisser, A. (1983). *The other side of silence: Sign language and the Deaf community in America.* New York: Alfred A. Knopf.

Nelson, K. (1996). *Language in cognitive development: The emergence of the mediated mind.* Cambridge, England: Cambridge University Press.

Nettle, D. (1999). *Linguistic diversity.* Oxford, England: Oxford University Press.

Nettle, D., & Romaine, S. (2000). *Vanishing voices: The extinction of the world's languages.* Oxford, England: Oxford University Press.

Nettleship, R. (1968). *The theory of education in the republic of Plato.* New York: Teachers College Press.

Newman, P. (2003). The endangered languages issue as a hopeless cause. In M. Janse & S. Tol (Eds.), *Language death and language maintenance* (pp. 1-13). Amsterdam: John Benjamins.

Nicaise, M., & Barnes, D. (1996). The union of technology, constructivism, and teacher education. *Journal of Teacher Education, 47,* 205-212.

Noddings, N. (1990). Constructivism in mathematics education. In R. Davis, C. Maher, & N. Noddings (Eds.), *Constructivist views on the teaching and learning of mathematics* (pp. 7-18). Reston, VA: National Council of Teachers of Mathematics.

Noddings, N. (1995). *Philosophy of education.* Boulder, CO: Westview Press.

Norlander-Case, K., Reagan, T., & Case, C. (1999). *The professional teacher: The preparation and nurturance of the reflective practitioner.* San Francisco: Jossey-Bass.

Nover, S. (1995). Politics and language: American Sign Language and English in deaf education. In C. Lucas (Ed.), *Sociolinguistics in deaf communities* (pp. 109-163). Washington, DC: Gallaudet University Press.

Nuessel, F. (1996). The symbolic nature of Esperanto. *Semiotica, 109,* 369-385.

Nuessel, F. (2000). *The Esperanto language.* New York: Legas.

Nyikos, M., & Hashimoto, R. (1997). Constructivist theory applied to collaborative learning in teacher education: In search of ZPD. *The Modern Language Journal, 81,* 506-517.

Obler, L., & Gjerlow, K. (1999). *Language and the brain.* Cambridge, England: Cambridge University Press.

O'Grady, W., & Dobrovolsky, M. (Eds.). (1996). *Contemporary linguistic analysis* (3rd ed.). Toronto: Copp Clark.

Okrand, M. (1992). *The Klingon dictionary.* New York: Pocket Books.

Omaggio Hadley, A. (2001). *Teaching language in context* (3rd ed.). Boston: Heinle & Heinle.

Ormrod, J. (1995). *Human learning* (2nd ed.). Englewood Cliffs, NJ: Prentice Hall.

Ortega, L. (1999). Language and equality: Ideological and structural constraints in foreign language education in the U.S. In T. Huebner & K. Davis (Eds.), *Sociopolitical perspectives on language policy and planning in the USA* (pp. 243-266). Amsterdam: John Benjamins.

Osborn, T. A. (1998). *The concept "foreignness" in U.S. secondary language curricula: A critical philosophical analysis.* Unpublished doctoral dissertation, University of Connecticut, Storrs.

Osborn, T. (2000). *Critical reflection and the foreign language classroom.* Westport, CT: Bergin & Garvey.

Osborn, T. (2003a). Market ideology, critical educational studies, and the image of foreign language education. *NECTFL Review, 52,* 41-46.

Osborn, T. (2003b). Not-so-foreign languages: The critical inquiry approach to moving beyond disciplines. In D. Kaufman, D. Moss & T. Osborn (Eds.), *Beyond the boundaries: A transdisciplinary approach to learning and teaching* (pp. 33-46). Westport, CT: Praeger.

Osborn, T. (2004). Corpus disciplinae? Toward a critical prognosis for contemporary language teacher preparation. In G. Bräuer & K. Sanders (Eds.), *New visions in foreign and second language education* (pp. 273-280). San Diego, CA: LARC Press.

Osborn, T. (in press). *Teaching world languages for social justice: A sourcebook of principles and practices.* Mahwah, NJ: Erlbaum.

Osborn, T., & Reagan, T. (1998). Why Johnny can't *hablar, parler,* or *sprechen:* Foreign language education and multicultural education. *Multicultural Education, 6,* 2-9.

Ovando, C. (1993). Language diversity and education. In J. Banks & C. McGee Banks (Eds.), *Multicultural education: Issues and perspectives* (2nd ed., pp. 215-235). Boston: Allyn & Bacon.

Ovando, C., Collier, V., & Combs, M. (2003). *Bilingual and ESL classrooms: Teaching in multicultural contexts* (3rd ed.). Boston: McGraw Hill.

Ovando, C., & Gourd, K. (1996). Knowledge construction, language maintenance, revitalization, and empowerment. In J. Banks (Ed.), *Multicultural education: Transformative knowledge and action.* New York: Teachers College Press.

Padden, C. (1980). The deaf community and the culture of deaf people. In C. Baker & R. Battison (Eds.), *Sign language and the deaf community* (pp. 89-103). Silver Spring, MD: National Association of the Deaf.

Padden, C., & Humphries, T. (1988). *Deaf in America: Voices from a culture.* Cambridge, MA: Harvard University Press.

Paget, R. (1951). *The new sign language.* London: The Welcome Foundation.

Parker, S. (1997). *Reflective teaching in the postmodern world: A manifesto for education in postmodernity.* Buckingham, UK: Open University Press.

Patton, M. (1978). *Utilization-focused evaluations.* Beverly Hills, CA: Sage.

Penn, C., & Reagan, T. (2001). Linguistic, social and cultural perspectives on sign language in South Africa. In E. Ridge, S. Makoni, & S. Ridge (Eds.), *Freedom and discipline: Essays in applied linguistics from Southern Africa* (pp. 49-65). New Delhi: Bahri.

Pennycook, A. (1994). *The cultural politics of English as an international language.* London: Longman.

Pennycook, A. (1995). English in the world/The world in English. In J. Tollefson (Ed.), *Power and inequality in language education* (pp. 34-58). Cambridge, England: Cambridge University Press.

Pennycook, A. (1998). *English and the discourses of colonialism.* London: Routledge.

Pennycook, A. (2000). The social politics and cultural politics of language classrooms. In J. Hall & W. Eggington (Eds.), *The sociopolitics of English language teaching* (pp. 89-103). Clevedon, England: Multilingual Matters.

Pennycook, A. (2001). *Critical applied linguistics: A critical introduction.* Mahwah, NJ: Erlbaum.

Peters, C. (2000). *Deaf American literature: From carnival to the canon.* Washington, DC: Gallaudet University Press.

Peters, R. S. (Ed.). (1967). *The concept of education.* London: Routledge & Kegan Paul.

Peters, R. S. (Ed.). (1973). *The philosophy of education.* Oxford, England: Oxford University Press.

Phillips, D. C. (1995). The good, the bad, and the ugly: The many faces of constructivism. *Educational Researcher, 24*, 5-12.

Phillips, D. C. (1996). Response to Ernst von Glasersfeld. *Educational Researcher, 25*, 20.

Phillips, D. C. (Ed.). (2000). *Constructivism in education: Opinions and second opinions on controversial issues: The Ninety-Ninth Yearbook of the National Society for the Study of Education, Part I.* Chicago: University of Chicago Press.

Phillips, J., & Terry, R. (Eds.). (1999). *Foreign language standards: Linking research, theories, and practices.* Lincolnwood, IL: National Textbook Co., in conjunction with the American Council on the Teaching of Foreign Languages.

Phillipson, R. (1988). Linguicism: Structures and ideologies in linguistic imperialism. In T. Skutnabb-Kangas & J. Cummins (Eds.), *Minority education: From shame to struggle* (pp. 339-358). Clevedon, England: Multilingual Matters.

Phillipson, R. (1992). *Linguistic imperialism.* Oxford, England: Oxford University Press.

Phillipson, R. (Ed.). (2000). *Rights to language: Equity, power, and education.* Mahwah, NJ: Erlbaum.

Phillipson, R. (2003). *English-only Europe? Challenging language policy.* London: Routledge.

Phillipson, R., Rannut, M., & Skutnabb-Kangas, T. (1995). Introduction. In T. Skutnabb-Kangas & R. Phillipson (Eds.), in collaboration with M. Rannut, *Linguistic human rights* (pp. 1-22). Berlin, Germany: Mouton de Gruyter.

Piaget, J. (1976). *Psychologie et epistémologie* [Psychology and epistemology]. Paris: Editions Gonthier.

Piaget, J. (1979). *L'epistémologie génétique* [Genetic epistemolog] (3rd ed.). Paris: Presses Universitaires de France.

Piaget, J. (1986). *Logique et connaissance scientifique* [Logic and scientific knowledge]. Paris: Gallimard.

Piaget, J. (1993). *Le jugement et le raisonnement chez l'enfant* [Judgment and reasoning in the child] (8th ed.). Paris: Delachaux & Niestle.

Piaget, J. (1996). *La construction du réel chez l'enfant* [The child's construction of reality] (6th ed.). Neuchatel: Delachaux & Niestle.

Pinker, S. (1994). *The language instinct: How the mind creates language.* New York: William Morrow.

Pinnock, P. (1994). *Xhosa: A cultural grammar for beginners.* Cape Town, South Africa: African Sun Press.

Piron, C. (1984). Contribution à l'étude des apports du yidiche à l'espéranto [Contribution to the study of the contributions of Yiddish to Esperanto]. *Jewish Language Review, 4,* 15-29.

Piron, C. (1989). Who are the speakers of Esperanto? In K. Schubert (Ed.), *Interlinguistics: Aspects of the science of planned languages* (pp. 157-172). Berlin, GErmany: Mouton de Gruyter.

Piron, C. (1991). *Esperanto: European or Asiatic language?* (Esperanto documents 22-A). Rotterdam: Universala Esperanto-Asocio.

Po-Ching, Yip, & Rimmington, D. (1997). *Chinese: An essential grammar.* London: Routledge.

Pool, J. (1987). Thinking about linguistic discrimination. *Language Problems and Language Planning, 11,* 3-21.

Posner, R. (1996). *The Romance languages.* Cambridge, England: Cambridge University Press.

Purves, D., Augustine, G., Fitzpatrick, D., Katz, L., LaMantia, A., & McNamara, J. (Eds.). (1997). *Neuroscience.* Sunderland, MA: Sinauer Associates.

Quick, M. (1989, May/June)). Does anyone here speak Esperanto? *Gifted Child Today,* 15-16.

Rainer, J., & Guyton, E. (1994). Developing a constructivist teacher education program: The policy-making stage. *Journal of Teacher Education, 45,* 140-146.

Ramsey, C. (1989). Language planning in deaf education. In C. Lucas (Ed.), *The sociolinguistics of the deaf community* (pp. 123-146). New York: Academic Press.

Reagan, T. (1985). The deaf as a linguistic minority: Educational considerations. *Harvard Educational Review, 55*(3), 265-277.

Reagan, T. (1990). Cultural considerations in the education of deaf children. In D. Moores & K. Meadow-Orlans (Eds.), *Educational and developmental aspects of deafness* (pp. 73-84). Washington, DC: Gallaudet University Press.

Reagan, T. (1992a). The deaf as a linguistic minority: Educational considerations. Reprinted in T. Hehir & T. Latus (Eds.), *Special education at the century's end: Evolution of theory and practice since 1970* (pp. 305-320). Cambridge, MA: Harvard Educational Review.

Reagan, T. (1992b, November 4-8). The debate about the status of ASL: A case study in cultural oppression. Paper presented at the annual meeting of the American Educational Studies Association, Pittsburgh, Pennsylvania.

Reagan, T. (1995a). "Neither easy to understand nor pleasing to see": The development of manual sign codes as language planning activity. *Language Problems and Language Planning, 19,* 133-150.

Reagan, T. (1995b). A sociocultural understanding of deafness: American Sign Language and the culture of deaf people. *International Journal of Intercultural Relations, 19,* 239-251.

Reagan, T. (1996). Bilingualism and the dual culture of the deaf. *South African Medical Journal, 86,* 797-799.

Reagan, T. (1997a). The case for applied linguistics in teacher education. *Journal of Teacher Education, 48,* 185-196.

Reagan, T. (1997b). When is a language not a language?: Challenges to "linguistic legitimacy" in educational discourse. *Educational Foundations, 11,* 5-28.

Reagan, T. (1998). Rejoinder to Vandenberg. *Educational Foundations, 12,* 87-90.

Reagan, T. (1999). Constructivist epistemology and second/foreign language pedagogy. *Foreign Language Annals, 32,* 413-425.

Reagan, T. (2000). But does it *count?* Reflections on "signing" as a foreign language. *NECTFL Review, 48,* 16-26.

Reagan, T. (2001a). The emancipatory power of language: Critical language awareness and the legacy of Clarence J. Karier. In K. Graves, T. Glander & C. Shea (Eds.), *Inexcusable omissions: Clarence Karier and the critical tradition in history of education scholarship* (pp. 245-262). New York: Peter Lang.

Reagan, T. (2001b). Language planning and policy. In. C. Lucas (Ed.), *The sociolinguistics of sign languages* (pp. 145-180). Cambridge, England: Cambridge University Press.

Reagan, T. (2002a). "Knowing" and "learning" a foreign language: Epistemological reflections on classroom practice. In T. Osborn (Ed.), *The future of foreign language education in the United States* (pp. 45-61). Westport, CT: Bergin & Garvey.

Reagan, T. (2002b). *Language, education and ideology: Mapping the linguistic landscape of U.S. schools.* Westport, CT: Praeger.

Reagan, T. (2002c). Teaching and learning sign language as a "foreign" language. *Journal for Language Teaching / Tydskrif vir Taalonderrig, 36,* 175-205.

Reagan, T. (2002d). Toward a political economy of the less commonly taught languages in the American public schools. In T. Osborn (Ed.) *The future of foreign language education in the U.S.* (pp. 125-138). Westport, CT: Bergin & Garvey.

Reagan, T., & Case, K. (1996). Linguistic pluralism for internationalization: The case for non-traditional approaches to language study for U.S. schools. In K. Müller (Ed.), *Language status in the post-Cold-War era* (pp. 97-107). Lanham, MD: University Press of America and the Center for Research and Documentation on World Language Problems.

Reagan, T., Case, C., & Brubacher, J. (2000). *Becoming a reflective educator: How to build a culture of inquiry in the schools* (2nd ed.). Thousand Oaks, CA: Corwin Press.

Reagan, T., & Díaz, E. (1996, May 3). Monolingual global education: The "flat earth" alternative. Paper presented at the Languages and Global Education Conference sponsored by the Center for Research and Documentation of World Language Problems and the Office of Conference Services at the United Nations.

Reagan, T., & Osborn, T. (1998). Power, authority and domination in foreign language education: Toward an analysis of educational failure. *Educational Foundations, 12,* 45-62.

Reagan, T., & Osborn, T. (2002). *The foreign language educator in society: Toward a critical pedagogy.* Mahwah, NJ: Erlbaum.

Reagan, T., & Vorster, J. (2000). Die politiek van vergetelheid: Stand van die minder-algemeen-onderrigte tale [The politics of oblivion: Situating the less commonly taught languages]. *Language Problems and Language Planning, 24,* 55-76.

Rhodes, N., & Branaman, L. (1999). *Foreign language instruction in the United States: A national survey of elementary and secondary schools.* McHenry, IL: Delta Systems and the Center for Applied Linguistics.

Richard-Amato, P. (1996). *Making it happen: Interaction in the second language classroom, from theory to practice.* White Plains, NY: Longman.

Richards, J., & Lockhart, C. (1994). *Reflective teaching in second language classrooms.* Cambridge, England: Cambridge University Press.

Richards, J., & Rodgers, T. (2001). *Approaches and methods in language teaching* (2nd ed.). Cambridge, England: Cambridge University Press.

Richardson, D. (1988). *Esperanto: Learning and using the international language.* Eastsound, WA: Esperanto League for North America, in cooperation with Orcas Publishing.

Richardson, V. (Ed.). (1997a). *Constructivist teacher education: Building a world of new understandings.* London: Falmer Press.

Richardson, V. (Ed.)(1997b). Constructivist teaching and teacher education: Theory and practice. In *Constructivist teacher education: Building a world of new understandings* (pp. 3-14). London: Falmer Press.

Rickford, J., & Rickford, R. (2000). *Spoken soul: The story of Black English.* New York: John Wiley.

Romaine, S. (2000). *Language in society: An introduction to sociolinguistics* (2nd ed.). Oxford, England: Oxford University Press.

Ryding, K. C. (1989). Less commonly taught languages: The current situation. In J. Alatis (Ed.), *Language teaching, testing, and technology* (pp. 114-121). Washington, DC: Georgetown University Press.

Sacks, O. (1989). *Seeing voices: A journey into the world of the deaf.* Berkeley: University of California Press.

Sadler, V., & Lins, U. (1972). Regardless of frontiers: A case study in linguistic persecution. In S. K. Ghosh (Ed.), *Man, language and society* (pp. 206-215). The Hague, The Netherlands: Mouton.

Safford, P., & Safford, E. (1996). *A history of childhood and disability.* New York: Teachers College Press.

Schein, J. (1989). *At home among strangers: Exploring the Deaf community in the United States.* Washington, DC: Gallaudet University Press.

Schein, J., & Stewart, D. (1995). *Language in motion: Exploring the nature of sign.* Washington, DC: Gallaudet University Press.

Schmitt, C., & Woodford, P. (1997). *Bienvendios: Glencoe Spanish 1.* New York: Glencoe (McGraw-Hill).

Schulz, R. (1988). Methods of teaching German in the United States: A historical perspective. In D. Benseler, W. Lohnes, & V. Nollendorfs (Eds.) *Teaching German in America: Prolegomena to a history* (pp. 55-75). Madison: University of Wisconsin Press.

Schwandt, T. (1994). Constructivist, interpretivist approaches to human inquiry. In N. Denzin & Y. Lincoln (Eds.), *Handbook of qualitative research* (pp. 118-137). Thousand Oaks, CA: Sage.

Searle, C. (1983). A common language. *Race and Class, 34,* 45-54.

Shapiro, J. (1993). *No pity: People with disabilities forging a new civil rights movement.* New York: Times Books.

Sherwood, B. (1982a). The educational value of Esperanto. In R. Eichloz & V. S. Eichloz (comps.), *Esperanto en la moderna mondo / Esperanto in the modern world* (pp. 408-413). Bailieboro, Ontario, Canada: Esperanto Press.

Sherwood, B. (1982b). Parol-sintezado aplikata al lingvo-instruado / Speech synthesis applied to language teaching. In R. Eichholz & V. S. Eichholz (comps.), *Esperanto en la moderna mondo/Esperanto in the modern world* (pp. 430-447). Bailieboro, Ontario, Canada: Esperanto Press.

Sherwood, B. (1983). *The educational value of Esperanto: An American view* (Esperanto documents 31-A). Rotterdam, The Netherlands: Universala Esperanto-Asocio.

Shrum, J., & Glisan, E. (1994). *Teacher's handbook: Contextualized language instruction.* Boston: Heinle and Heinle.

Sinclair, H., Berthoud, I., Gerard, J. & Venesiano, E. (1985). Constructivisme et psycholinguistique génétique [Constructivism and genetic psycholinguistics]. *Archives de Psychologie, 53,* 37-60.

Skutnabb-Kangas, T. (1988). Multilingualism and the education of minority children. In T. Skutnabb-Kangas & J. Cummins (Eds.), *Minority education: From shame to struggle* (pp. 9-44). Clevedon, England: Multilingual Matters.

Skutnabb-Kangas, T. (1994). Linguistic human rights: A prerequisite for bilingualism. In I. Ahlgren & K. Hyltenstam (Eds.), *Bilingualism in deaf education* (pp. 139-159). Hamburg, Germany: Signum Press.

Skutnabb-Kangas, T. (2000). *Linguistic genocide in education—Or worldwide diversity and human rights?* Mahwah, NJ: Erlbaum.

Skutnabb-Kangas, T., & Bucak, S. (1995). Killing a mother tongue: How the Kurds are deprived of linguistic human rights. In T. Skutnabb-Kangas & R. Phillipson, in conjunction with M. Rannut (Eds.), *Linguistic human rights: Overcoming linguistic discrimination* (pp. 347-370). Berlin, Germany: Mouton de Gruyter.

Skutnabb-Kangas, T., & Phillipson, R., in collaboration with M. Rannut. (Eds.). (1995). *Linguistic human rights: Overcoming linguistic discrimination.* Berlin, Germany: Mouton de Gruyter.

Slattery, P., & Rapp, D. (2003). *Ethics and the foundations of education: Teaching convictions in a postmodern world.* Boston: Allyn & Bacon.

Smith, J. (1999). *Essentials of early English.* London: Routledge.

Smith, N. (2002). *Language, bananas and bonobos: Linguistic problems, puzzles and polemics.* Oxford, England: Blackwell.

Smyth, D. (2002). *Thai: An essential grammar.* London: Routledge.

Soder, R. (Ed.). (1996). *Democracy, education, and the schools.* San Francisco, CA: Jossey-Bass.

Solso, R. (Ed.). (1997). *Mind and brain sciences in the 21st century.* Cambridge, MA: MIT Press.

Sonnabend, H. (1979). *Esperanto: Lerneja eksperimento* [Esperanto: An educational experiment]. Pisa, Italy: Edistudio.

Sonntag, S. (2003). *The local politics of global English: Case studies in linguistic globalization.* Lanham, MD: Lexington Books.

Spener, D. (1991). Transitional bilingual education and the socialization of immigrants. In M. Minami & B. Kennedy (Eds.), *Language issues in literacy and bilingual/multicultural education* (pp. 424-446). Cambridge, MA: Harvard Educational Review.

Spivey, N. (1997). *The constructivist metaphor: Reading, writing and the making of meaning.* San Diego, CA: Academic Press.

Spolsky, B. (1989). *Conditions for second language learning.* Oxford, England: Oxford University Press.

Steffe, L., Cobb, P., & von Glasersfeld, E. (1988). *Construction of arithmetical meanings and strategies.* New York: Springer-Verlag.

Steffe, L., & Gale, J. (Eds.). (1995). *Constructivism in education.* Hillsdale, NJ: Erlbaum.

Stevens, E., Wood, G., & Sheehan, J. (2002). *Justice, ideology and education* (4th ed.). Boston: McGraw Hill.

Stewart, D., & Akamatsu, C. T. (1988). The coming of age of American Sign Language. *Anthropology and Education Quarterly, 19,* 235-252.

Stillman, R. (1995). *The new philosophy and universal languages in seventeenth-century England: Bacon, Hobbes, and Wilkins.* London: Bucknell University Press.

Stokoe, W. (Ed.). (1980). *Sign and culture: A reader for students of American Sign Language.* Silver Spring, MD: Linstok Press.

Stokoe, W. (1993). *Sign language structures.* Silver Spring, MD: Linstok Press. (Original work published 1960)

Strike, K., Haller, E., & Soltis, J. (1988). *The ethics of school administration.* New York: Teachers College Press.

Strike, K., &. Soltis, J. (1998). *The ethics of teaching* (3rd ed.). New York: Teachers College Press.

Sutton-Spence, R., & Woll, B. (1998). *The linguistics of British Sign Language: An introduction.* Cambridge, England: Cambridge University Press.

Sylwester, R. (1995). *A celebration of neurons: An educator's guide to the human brain.* Alexandria, VA: Association for Supervision and Curriculum Development.

Symoens, E. (1989). *The socio-political, educational and cultural roots of Esperanto.* Antwerpen, Belgium: Internacia Ligo de Esperantistaj Instruistoj.

Szerdahelyi, I. (1966). Esperanto et propédeutique linguistique [Esperanto and linguistic propaedeutics]. *Langues Modernes, 60,* 255-259.

Szerdahelyi, I. (1975). La internacia pedagogia-didaktika eksperimento kvinlanda: La rezultoj de la unua mezurado [The international five-country experiment: Initial results]. In H. Behrmann (Ed.), *Lehrplanerische Rationalisierung des Sprachunterrichts* [Curricular rationale for language teaching]. Paderborn, Germany: Institut für Kybernetische Pädagogik.

Szerdahelyi, I., & Frank, H. (1976). Zur pädagogischer Bestimmung relativer Schwierigkeiten verschiedener Sprachen [Toward the pedagogical classification of relative learning difficulties in different languages]. *Grundlagenstudien aus Kybernetik und Geisteswissenschaft, 17,* 39-44.

Thagard, P. (1996). *Mind: Introduction to cognitive science.* Cambridge, MA: MIT Press.

Thomas, L., & Wareing, S. (1999). *Language, society and power.* London: Routledge.

Thomas, U. (1988). Mark Twain's German language learning experiences. In D. Benseler, W. Lohnes, & V. Nollendorfs (Eds.) *Teaching German in America: Prolegomena to a history* (pp. 133-143). Madison: University of Wisconsin Press.

Tobin, K. (Ed.). (1993). *The practice of constructivism in science education.* Hillsdale, NJ: Erlbaum.

Todorov, T. (1969). *Grammaire du Décaméron* [Grammar of the Décameron]. The Hague, Netherlands: Mouton.

Tollefson, J. (1991). *Planning language, planning inequality: Language policy in the community.* London: Longman.

Tollefson, J. (Ed.). (1995). *Power and inequality in language education.* Cambridge, England: Cambridge University Press.

Tonkin, H. (1977). *Esperanto and international language problems: A research bibliography* (4th ed.). Washington, DC: Esperantic Studies Foundation.

Tonkin, H. (1988, April 16). *Beyond the competitive edge: The peaceful uses of language study.* Keynote address, Annual Conference of the California Foreign Language Teachers Association.

Tonkin, H. (Ed.). (1997). *Esperanto, interlinguistics, and planned languages.* Lanham, MD: University Press of America.

Tonkin, H., & Fettes, M. (1996). *Esperanto studies: An overview* (Esperanto documents 43-A). Rotterdam, The Netherlands: Universala Esperanto-Asocio.

Tonkin, H., & Reagan, T. (Eds.). (2003). *Language in the twenty-first century.* Amsterdam: John Benjamins.

Tozer, S., Violas, P., & Senese, G. (1998). *School and society: Historical and contemporary perspectives* (3rd ed.). Boston: McGraw Hill.

Trueba, H. (1991). The role of culture in bilingual instruction: Linking linguistic and cognitive development. In O. Garcia (Ed.), *Bilingual education: Focusschrift in honor of Joshua A. Fishman on the occasion of his 65th birthday* (Vol. 1, pp. 43-55). Amsterdam: John Benjamins.

Twain, M. (1966). *The innocents abroad.* New York: Signet Classics. (Original work published 1869)

Ur, P. (1996). *A course in language teaching: Practice and theory.* Cambridge, England: Cambridge University Press.

Valdés, G. (1981). Pedagogical implications of teaching Spanish to the Spanish-speaking in the United States. In G. Valdés, A. Lozano, & R. García-Moya (Eds.), *Teaching Spanish to the Hispanic bilingual: Issues, aims and methods* (pp. 3-20). New York: Teachers College Press.

Valli, C., & Lucas, C. (2000). *Linguistics of American Sign Language: An introduction* (3rd ed.). Washington, DC: Gallaudet University Press.

Vandenberg, D. (1998). A response to Reagan. *Educational Foundations, 12,* 83-85.

Van Hoorde, J. (1998). Let Dutch die? Over the Taalunie's dead body. *InfoNT, 2,* 6-10.

van Lier, L. (1995). *Introducing language awareness.* London: Penguin English.

van Lier, L. (1996). *Interaction in the language curriculum: Awareness, autonomy and authenticity.* London: Longman.

von Glasersfeld, E. (1984). An introduction to radical constructivism. In P. Watzlawick (Ed.), *The invented reality: How do we know what we believe we know?* (pp. 17-40). New York: Norton.

von Glasersfeld, E. (1989). Cognition, construction of knowledge, and teaching. *Synthese, 80,* 121-140.

von Glasersfeld, E. (1993). Questions and answers about radical constructivism. In K. Tobin (Ed.), *The practice of constructivism in science education* (pp. 23-38). Hillsdale, NJ: Erlbaum.

von Glasersfeld, E. (1995a). A constructivist approach to teaching. In L. Steffe & J. Gale (Eds.), *Constructivism in education* (pp. 3-15). Hillsdale, NJ: Erlbaum.

von Glasersfeld, E. (1995b). *Radical constructivism: A way of knowing.* London: Falmer Press.

von Glasersfeld, E. (1996). Footnotes to "The many faces of constructivism." *Educational Researcher, 25,* 19.

Vygotsky, L. (1978). *Mind in society: The development of higher psychological processes.* Cambridge, MA: Harvard University Press.

Vygotsky, L. (1986). *Thought and language.* Cambridge, MA: MIT Press. (Original work published 1934)

Walker, G. (1989). The less commonly taught languages in the context of American pedagogy. In H. Lepke (Ed.), *Shaping the future: Challenges and opportunities* (pp. 111-137). Middlebury, VT: Northeast Conference on the Teaching of Foreign Languages.

Walker, G. (1991). Gaining place: The less commonly taught languages in American schools. *Foreign Language Annals, 24,* 131-150.

Wallace, C. (1997). The role of language awareness in critical pedagogy. In L. van Lier & D. Corson (Eds.), *Encyclopedia of language and education: Vol. 6. Knowledge about language* (pp. 241-249). Dordrecht, The Netherlands: Kluwer.

Wallinger, L. (Ed.). (2002). *Teaching in changing times: The courage to lead.* Boston: McGraw-Hill.

Walton, A. R. (1992). *Expanding the vision of foreign language education: Enter the less commonly taught languages.* NFLC Occasional Papers. Washington, DC: National Foreign Language Center.

Walworth, M., Moores, D., & O'Rourke, T. J. (Eds.). (1992). *A free hand: Enfranchising the education of deaf children.* Silver Spring, MD: T. J.

Wardhaugh, R. (1987). *Languages in competition: Dominance, diversity, and decline.* Oxford, England: Basil Blackwell, in association with André Deutsch.

Wardhaugh, R. (1999). *Proper English: Myths and misunderstandings about language.* Oxford, England: Blackwell.

Watzke, J. (2003). *Lasting change in foreign language education: A historical case for change in national policy.* Westport, CT: Praeger.

Wei, L. (Ed.). (2000). *The bilingualism reader.* London: Routledge.

Wells, J. (1989). *Lingvistikaj aspektoj de Esperanto* [Linguistic aspects of Esperanto]. Rotterdam, The Netherlands: Universala Esperanto-Asocio.

Widdowson, H. G. (1998). Skills, abilities, and contexts of reality. *Annual Review of Applied Linguistics, 18,* 323-333.

Wilcox, S. (1987). Breaking through the culture of silence. *Sign Language Studies, 55,* 163-174.

Wilcox, S. (Ed.). (1988). Academic acceptance of American Sign Language [Special issue]. *Sign Language Studies,* No. 59.

Wilcox, S. (Ed.). (1989). *American deaf culture.* Burtonsville, MD: Linstok Press.

Wilcox, S., & Wilcox, P. (1997). *Learning to see: Teaching American Sign Language as a second language* (2nd ed.). Washington, DC: Gallaudet University Press.

Wilkinson, L., & Janks, H. (1998). Teaching direct and reported speech from a critical language awareness (CLA) perspective. *Educational Review, 50,* 181-190.

Williams, C. (Ed.). (1991). *Linguistic minorities: Society and territory.* Clevedon, England: Multilingual Matters.

Williams, M., & Burden, R. (1997). *Psychology for language teachers: A social constructivist approach.* Cambridge, England: Cambridge University Press.

Williams, N. (1965). A language teaching experiment. *Canadian Modern Language Review, 22,* 26-28.

Winitzky, N., & Kauchak, D. (1997). Constructivism in teacher education: Applying cognitive theory to teacher learning. In V. Richardson (Ed.), *Constructivist teacher education: Building a world of new understandings* (pp. 59-83). London: Falmer Press.

Wink, J. (2000). *Critical pedagogy: Notes from the real world* (2nd ed.). New York: Longman.

Winston, E. (Ed.). (1999). *Storytelling and conversation: Discourse in deaf communities.* Washington, DC: Gallaudet University Press.

Wittgenstein, L. (1961). *Tractatus logico-philosophicus.* London: Routledge & Kegan Paul.

Wittgenstein, L. (1974). *Philosophical grammar.* Berkeley: University of California Press.

Wittgenstein, L. (1980). *Culture and value.* Chicago: University of Chicago Press. (Original work pubished 1946)

Wolff, H. E. (2000). Language and society. In B. Heine & D. Nurse (Eds.), *African languages: An introduction* (pp. 298-347). Cambridge, England: Cambridge University Press.

Woll, B., Sutton-Spence, R., & Elton, F. (2001). Multilingualism: The global approach to sign languages. In C. Lucas (Ed.), *The sociolinguistics of sign languages* (pp. 8-32). Cambridge, England: Cambridge University Press.

Wood, R. (1975). Teaching the interlanguage: Some experiments. *Lektos: Interdisciplinary Working Papers in Language Sciences* (Special issue, Papers from the Seminar on Interlinguistics, Modern Language Association). Louisville, KY: University of Louisville.

Wood, R. (1982). *Current work in the linguistics of Esperanto* (Esperanto documents 28-A). Rotterdam, The Netherlands: Universala Esperanto-Asocio.

Wood, T., Cobb, P., & Yackel, E. (1995). Reflections of learning and teaching mathematics in elementary school. In L. Steffe & J. Gale (Eds.), *Constructivism in education* (pp. 401-422). Hillsdale, NJ: Erlbaum.

Woods, D. (1996). *Teacher cognition in language teaching: Beliefs, decision-making and classroom practice.* Cambridge, England: Cambridge University Press.

Woodward, J. (1982). *How you gonna get to heaven if you can't talk with Jesus: On depathologizing Deafness.* Silver Spring, MD: T. J.

Wrigley, O. (1997). *The politics of deafness.* Washington, DC: Gallaudet University Press.

Zamel, V., & Spack, R. (Eds.). (2002). *Enriching ESOL pedagogy.* Mahwah, NJ: Erlbaum.

Zamenhof, L. (1963). *Fundamento de Esperanto* [The foundation of Esperanto]. Maramande, France: Esperantaj Francaj Eldonoj. (Original work published 1905)

Zeichner, K., & Liston, D. (1996). *Reflective teaching: An introduction.* Mahwah, NJ: Erlbaum.

Zietsman, A. (1996). Constructivism: Super theory for all educational ills? *South African Journal of Higher Education, 10,* 70-75.

Zotwana, S. (1991). *Xhosa in context: From novice to intermediate.* Cape Town, South Africa: Perskor.

Printed in the United States
R1422900001B/R14229PG31305LVSX00002B/2}

9 781593 113346